M000020536

BRENDA L. THOMAS

laying down my burdens

a memoir

laying down my burdens
a memoir

Phillywriter.com, LLC
PO Box 39111
Philadelphia, PA 19136

A note to my readers:
The subject matter of this memoir is not intended to be offensive, but to adequately depict the serious nature of domestic violence. It is not a work of journalism; the only claim I make regarding interchanges with the people portrayed here is that those interchanges are recreations of my own emotions and memories. All I know is that these are the words and incidents that so many years later resound in my memory.

Disclaimer:
In order to protect the privacy of certain individuals in this book, names and other identifying characteristics have been changed.

All rights reserved, including the right to reproduce this book or portions thereof in any form whatsoever. For information contact Phillywriter.com, LLC, PO Box 39111, Philadelphia, PA 19136, or brendalthomas@comcast.net.

Editor: Leigh Karsch and Matt Cordes
Art Direction: Leigh Karsch
Interior Design: Shawna A. Grundy
Cover Photography: Dominic Episcopo
Fashion Stylist: Kelisha L. Rawlinson
Hair Stylist: Brandy Smith
Makeup: Monica Bush

First Edition September 2007
ISBN 13: 978-0-9797622-0-8
ISBN 10: 0-9797622-0-8

Also by Brenda L. Thomas

Every Woman's Got a Secret

The Velvet Rope

Fourplay...the dance of sensuality

Threesome: Where Seduction Power and Basketball Collide

Kiss the Year Goodbye
(with Crystal Lacey Winslow, Tu-Shonda L. Whitaker &
Daaimah S. Poole)

Four Degrees of Heat
(with Crystal Lacey Winslow, Rochelle Allers &
ReShonda Tate Billingsley)

Published by Pocket Books a division of Simon & Schuster, Inc.

DEDICATION

*To my children, Kelisha L. and Kelvin J.
for all that I've put you through—hoping that this
provides understanding and reason
to why I do the things I do.
Remember: when you're not focused on God,
He's focused on you.*

*I love you,
Mom*

Why I Published This Book

For as long as I've been writing this memoir, so many times and for so many reasons, I've changed my mind about publishing it. It was one hot Saturday afternoon in June of 2007 when it all came together. I was watching 13 little girls whose names I didn't know perform praise dancing in the park. I was all smiles until I wondered—actually I knew—that one of them would silently suffer under the hands of an abuser, and yet another would be stalked and killed. That statistic frightened me. However, what brought the reality even closer to my heart and caused me to leave the audience was the thought of my three innocent granddaughters, Jazzlyn, Briana and Jada falling victim to the same violence.

It was during that array of emotions when I realized that in order for them to hear the silent cries of domestic violence it was their Ganny's story that needed to be the loudest. Hence, I decided at that moment that I had to share my story, no matter what the cost to me personally.

Jazzlyn, Briana and Jada, please remember to love and respect yourselves more than anyone else ever could.

Acknowledgements

Thank you God for listening to the prayers of my parents, Thurmond and Mary Thomas. It was their prayers that gave me the backbone to survive this journey somewhere having found the self-respect and values they'd taught me.

I give thanks to Kim Gerald, my best friend in the whole wide world, for encouraging me to share my story of survival with the world. Renee Washington, if only I'd taken heed to your story I wouldn't have to write my own. My friend, Leigh Karsch, God bless her for taking on so many roles to bring this memoir to fruition. Maurice Carter, my son-in-law, without you we'd never be turning these pages. But there are those special friends who've been with me through the years when I was far from the person I am now, friends who gave me love in spite of my insecurities: Sharon Woodridge, Denise Robinson, Carmen Carrion, and the hardest working women in the book business, Nakea Murray, Pamela Artis, and Tiarra Giddings. However, my *friend* Darryl Grant has been the person with more confidence in my success than I have and he continues to encourage me as if writing this book were second nature.

Then there are my siblings: my big brother Joe, who assisted in spoiling me, and his children Jodi, Eric, Nate and Nanette; and always the memory of the angel on my shoulder, my sister Gwennie whose children Eric, Erika, Trisha and Tiana continue to carry on her spirit; my brother Gregory and his sons, Cooker, Michael, Terrell, Jeffery, and Kyle, who promise to protect me; and my free-spirited brother Jeffery and his children; Jeffery, Kamille, Ivy, Sissy, Spencer and Lilanya. There are also people who've brought a little something extra to my life, Theresa Thomas, and Barbara and Chris Payne.

To those who carry on the spirit of my ancestors: my Aunts, Ruth, Rubynell, Liz, and Martha, and Uncles Leroy, and Richard. And of course I wouldn't be complete without my extended family of aunts, uncles, nephews, nieces and cousins, I love you all.

Contents

Contents

laying down my burdens
a memoir

Begin each day as if it were on purpose.
~ ~Anonymous

prologue

He was spending the weekend with me at my parents' while they were down the shore. I'd gone to the store with our three-year-old daughter, Kelisha, to get milk and all I can do is imagine how he made his discovery.

He'd probably decided to make the bed and while he was tucking the sheets in between the mattress and box spring, his hand hit what felt like a book—my journal, filled with scraps of paper. I would hope that once he pulled it out from its hiding place he hesitated in opening it. I would like to believe that he initially thought to himself, *"This must be her personal journal; I can't read this."*

He knew writing was important to me, whether it was poems that I wrote to him confessing my love, or journal entries of my hopes of one day becoming an author. I'm guessing, though, that his curiosity to learn more about my inner thoughts proved too strong, leaving him no choice but to open the pages to my life and begin reading thoughts that I'd dare not tell anybody but myself.

I can see him sitting there where I found him, reading about how much I loved him and how badly I wanted our relationship to work out. I'd written about how hurt I was that he had another girlfriend with whom he was spending most of his time. But something tells me he ignored that, and probably passed over my accounts of how I had tried to understand his abusive nature—from the first time he pushed me over the bed to the punches and chokeholds I'd learned to endure.

No, something tells me he focused on how I'd written about the man who'd become my confidant, who I would talk to when I came to work battered from his anger, the man who refused to believe those bruises were from a slammed door or playing on the floor with my daughter. He was the man who encouraged me to leave and the man who'd taken me in his arms one afternoon in a dirty vacant office at our workplace.

I had written: *"I wanted to see you and kiss you," he said smiling. So we stood there, me in a white dress and him pressed against me in his dirty work clothes.*

With his arms firmly wrapped around me, he slowly moved his hands around my waist and under my dress. His tongue was deep in my mouth, while his fingers made their way under my panties. Had it not been for where we were, I might've let him have his way.

Reaching the top of the stairs, I first hear the rustle of papers. My heart stops and starts again. My mouth is dry and I force my legs to move toward the back bedroom. Bracing myself, I step through the bedroom doorway.

"Russell, please don't read those. They're personal."

He doesn't answer.

I hold out my hand, "Please, can't you just give them to me?"

"Fuck no!" he says, his voice a low rumble.

"But Russell they're—his sharp glare cuts off my words.

Knowing I can't simply snatch away from him what belongs to me, I feel the need to quickly busy myself in order to come to terms with what's happening. I snap into autopilot and figure that by focusing on breakfast I can pretend that what I know is about to happen might be delayed if only for the seven minutes it takes to fry bacon and scramble eggs.

I back out the doorway and go downstairs to the kitchen. Our daughter is the only one who will eat. Meanwhile, Russell skulks down the steps and sits on the couch, refusing to acknowledge my presence. Needing to talk to someone besides me, he phones his mother, Eve, revealing to her the details of my writing.

I sit his plate of food on the coffee table in front of him, his grits stiffen and the bacon continues to shrivel while he talks to his mother. Absentmindedly he pushes the plate away.

To distract my daughter I turn on the cartoons but also keep an ear to his conversation as he reads parts of my journal entries to Eve. I know from the creases across his forehead and the redness that fills his cheeks that it's paining him. I'm also aware that Russell's talking to his mother in no way assures me that she will have my best interest at heart, but still I pray that she can somehow console him. Finally, he tells her he's going to see her in a few minutes and hangs up the phone. He takes my journals with him. I want to ask him to leave them behind. Why does he need them? Is it because he's going to destroy them? That wouldn't bother me as much as the thought of him consumed by the idea of another man's hands on my body.

Not much later Russell calls me from a phone booth. This is the call I should ignore, the one that will bury part of my life for 10 years.

"Brenda, can you come over to my house? I wanna talk," he says, his voice full of sadness instead of anger.

"Okay," I say, feeling guilty and hoping I can make him understand why I'd reached out to another man.

There is nobody for me to leave Kelisha with, so I take her along with me to meet him at the bus stop. We ride the 66 trolley, the El train and the 52 bus mostly in silence, until we arrive at his house on 52nd and Viola Streets.

He beckons for me and Kelisha to follow him upstairs. The narrow middle bedroom is small and hot, the air conditioner not providing much relief from the sweltering July heat. The room is only big enough for his queen-sized bed, a dresser and chest, on top of which sits his 19" television.

He tells Kelisha to sit on the bed and play with her dolls. Russell then props himself against the headboard and proceeds to read my journal aloud. I can tell he is doing it to intimidate me. He wants to hurt me with my own words.

With his voice in the background, I take in the close quarters

3

of the room. His dust-filled dresser is littered with products: Right Guard deodorant, Ultra Sheen hair grease, Pierre Cardin cologne and the wire pick for his hair. Sticking out from under the bed is an old turntable and a Stacy Adams shoebox filled with cassette tapes.

He has yet to acknowledge me, so I keep my distance by situating myself next to the window where I fold my arms across my chest so he won't see me trembling.

At his next pause, I interrupt. "Russell, I'm sorry you found those. It's not what you think."

He snaps his head in my direction and I can see beads of perspiration forming on his top lip—this tells me it would be best if I keep quiet. I glance over at Kelisha who is twisting her dolls' hair in knots.

He finally addresses me.

"Brenda, why would you write this shit? I mean, how could you let a man stick his dirty finger in you?"

"Russell, you don't understand."

"I understand alright, you ain't shit, *everybody* told me that. Why aren't you any fuckin' good?"

I shrug my shoulders as if to say, "I don't know why at the age of 23 I am considered no good."

"When did you start fucking this nigga, Brenda?"

"I didn't. It wasn't like that."

"That's bullshit. Don't no man feel sorry for your ass, he just wanted some pussy. You fucked him in that dirty room, didn't you?"

Between quivering lips I say, "No Russell, I swear I didn't."

I try to answer his questions, but rather than listen he continues to berate me about how I'm no good.

"Why you standing all way over there?"

Again, I shrug my shoulders and play dumb, knowing I'm there to stay out of striking distance.

"You love that nigga don't you?" he asks.

I move to the corner, trying to position myself behind the TV.

"I love *you* Russell. I don't love nobody else."

4

He moves from the bed so quickly that I don't have a chance to defend myself.

WHAM! He slaps me on the side of my head.

"Tell me the fuckin' truth, Brenda!"

Protecting my face with my hands I whine, "I am, I am, I swear I am."

I look over his shoulder at our daughter, who is busy in her own world. She is scared, I'm sure, to even glance at the monster her father has become.

With all 6'3" of him hovering over me, I take every slap, punch and kick he deals me. I take them because I am guilty of being all the names he shouts: slut, whore, dirty bitch. None of it, however, hurts as much as knowing that my daughter is a witness to his violent attack.

I cover my mouth to keep from shrieking, but I hear my daughter's frightened voice, "Mommy?"

When she starts to cry because she can't ignore us anymore he yells, "Lay down and go to sleep!"

I want to yell, "How can she? It's six o'clock in the evening!"

Hysterically, I cry to him. "Please don't hit me anymore, Russell. I'm begging you."

"You don't think you deserve it?" he asks.

I relent. "Yes."

He backs me up against the window. The air conditioner knobs dig into my skin.

"Well then, shut the fuck up and take it!"

"Russell, you don't have to beat me in front of Kelisha."

"Why not? She needs to know what a dirty bitch you are," he says.

He steps back across the room and bends over to get his sneakers. I pray he is going to take a walk to cool off. Instead, he flings a hi-top red and white Adidas in my direction, hitting me between the breasts.

I don't know who cries the loudest, my daughter or I.

"Stop it Daddy! You're hurting my Mommy!"

He turns to Kelisha and shouts, "Git your ass in the room with Tank!"

She scurries off the bed and out the door to where his younger brother is lying, recovering from five gunshot wounds he received two weeks ago as a result of his criminal lifestyle.

Having retrieved the sneaker, Russell whips around. "Take your clothes off!"

For the first time in our five-year relationship I am terrified. I have never been the one to hurt him; his beatings in the past were always in response to my accusing him of being with other women, or my talking back to him. This time, though, it is clearly my fault. I am guilty of having been intimate with another man.

I do as I'm told and undress down to my bra and panties. This is usually when he forces me to have sex and is the only way he calms down. So I am submissive because in the past it has meant the punishment will soon come to an end.

"Sit your ass down!"

My eyes follow his hand gripping the sneaker as my mind scrambles to think of something more I can do—something that will keep him from hitting me. The words won't come fast enough. "Can't you just listen to me?" I beg.

He pounds the sneaker across my thighs.

"You better tell me the fucking truth! You fucked that nigga, didn't you?"

"No, no," I holler out, my hands flailing in front of me. I'm not quick enough, because the sole of the Adidas smacks across my face. I can see blood splashed on his shirt and feel its wetness on my cheek.

Through my dulled senses I hear footsteps dragging down the hall. I pray it is Tank coming to save me. There is a knock at the door. It opens and it is him.

He looks at us, shakes his head and says to Russell, "Com'on, smoke a joint man and cool out."

Russell answers, "I'll be in," before giving me one last look of disgust and exiting the room.

With Russell gone from the room I consider running, but there is no escaping—especially without my daughter. My God what could she be thinking?

Whispering, I pray to God that the sharp pangs I feel in my

back and stomach aren't from a broken rib. The shock of his beating reels in my head. In the past I'd just go numb, but now I was wide awake, thinking that this might just be the one to put him over the edge. Maybe this time he would really kill me. Yes he's beaten me before, but this time *he's* hurting from something I've written.

I glance down at the journal pages strewn across the floor. Now that he has discovered my journal and my infidelity my writing will no longer be a comfort for me. It is the only thing that gives me optimism about having a better life, even when the world around me is spinning out of control. It's as if once I write it down it has happened to someone else.

I rise from the bed. Seeing my reflection in the mirror I realize I'm looking at a woman I don't recognize. I have no idea how I got to the point where I would allow a man to beat me. I stare at myself in disbelief, trying to get a grip on what might lay ahead.

Ten minutes later Russell returns to find me sitting on the bed, my knees to my chest. I am clenching my ankles, rocking back and forth.

"Stand your dirty ass up!"

Once again I do as I'm told. He picks up his sneaker from the top of the television to finish what he had started. Moments later I'm slumped beside the dresser.

"Tell me something," he says, crouching down in front me. His voice is a whisper.

I stare up at him, hoping he'll have mercy on me.

"Why you always writing some dirty shit?" he asks, his face so close to mine I can smell the joint on his breath.

"I don't know."

"I'm gonna promise you something Brenda; if you ever write some shit like this again, it's gonna be the last time."

His hands grip my wrists tightly. His knuckles are red.

"No, you don't understand. I swear, Brenda. Your shit is so fucked up that you better not *ever* write, keep a journal, none of that shit or I'm gonna kill you. You hear me?" The tone of his voice is so low, so deliberate, it sends shivers through me.

"I won't," I promise, as the imprint of the sneaker brands

my soul, severing my desire to write, replacing it with a paralyzing fear.

"I swear, I *promise* you Brenda—I'll kill your dumb ass. You understand?"

I lower my head like a dog that's been disciplined.

"Now suck my dick."

chapter one

A Fresh Start
August, 1982

After six tumultuous years, God knows we needed a new beginning. This was our chance to get away from the madness in Philly that weighed down our relationship. I'd found a job opportunity for Russell at Rutherford Steel in Charlotte, North Carolina, sent in his resume and they'd called and hired him right over the phone.

I was working as a secretary through a temp agency and collecting unemployment, so relocating wasn't a problem.

Kelisha was four years old and would be ready for kindergarten in September. This would be the perfect time for her to adjust to a new environment, and an opportunity for her to grow up in the quiet of the country as opposed to the gritty streets of Logan.

The plan was for Russell to travel down there alone to get started with the job and find us a place to live. The company was giving him a two-week stay at the Holiday Inn. I paid to get his van in shape for the road, bought him food, even found him some work clothes—I did anything I could to help him get started at his new job.

Least excited about our move were our families. My parents, La-La and Pop-Pop, had never been thrilled about our relationship to begin with, and they had good reason. They felt the last thing I needed to do was leave town, especially with their granddaughter. Russell's family simply felt I wanted to take him away from them.

But that's why we were leaving, to get that fresh start and to prove to everyone—including ourselves—that this relationship could work.

The night before his departure, with Kelisha at my parent's house, Russell and I had our own private bon voyage party. We smoked joints and made toasts with Asti Spumante, all in anticipation of our new life. After we'd gotten pretty high I put all of my energy into showing Russell how much I loved him, giving him something to remember on those lonely nights in Charlotte without me.

The following morning while Russell packed his clothes and made phone calls to get his things in order, I did what any good woman would do: I busied myself frying chicken, mixing potato salad and filling his cooler with cold Pepsi's. His road companion for the 10-hour trip was going to be Bear, our black Chow-Chow.

That night I went to bed anxiously awaiting his arrival call, but by the time I woke up the next morning I hadn't heard from him. I didn't want to panic but thought that something had gone wrong. Maybe he'd been in an accident and they didn't know whom to contact. Or worse yet, maybe some rednecks had strung him up. I mean he *was* headed south.

I dialed the operator in Charlotte to get the number for the Holiday Inn. Upon reaching the hotel I asked if Russell Douglass had checked in, and they transferred my call to his room.

"Hello," a woman answered.

"Yes, can I speak to Russell?" I asked, surprised that a woman would be answering the phone in his room.

"Hold on," she said.

Instead of Russell picking up, the line went dead.

Naturally, I assumed they'd put me through to the wrong room. I hung up and redialed. The desk put me through again.

"Hello?" I heard Russell ask.

"Russell, I just called there and some girl answered the

phone."

"What? You must've dialed the wrong room."

"Well she acted like you were there."

"Brenda, who would be here with me? They must've put you through to the wrong room," he insisted, making me feel foolish.

"Maybe, but . . . why didn't you call me when you got in?" I asked changing the subject.

"Man, by the time I got down here it was late and I was dead tired. I went right to sleep."

"So, what's it like down there?"

"It's okay. It's quiet as shit."

"You think you gonna like it?"

"I don't know, but look I gotta go 'cause I have to get over to the job. I'll call you later," he said, rushing me off the phone.

"Alright, I love you Russell."

"Yeah, I love you too."

I heard from him about every two days. Most times he called me collect but I didn't mind. Hell, I didn't even mind when he'd called complaining that he'd run out of money, so I wired him $100. Russell told me the job was going well, that he'd already met some friends and yes, Charlotte would be the place for us to make our new start. He'd even begun looking at apartments and houses for us to rent. This assured me that he was serious about our new life and that the focus would be on me, him and Kelisha. For so long, I had hoped for this fresh start, away from the party life and from the constant threat of Russell's infidelity.

I began to put into motion my plans to move Kelisha and me to North Carolina. There was packing to be done, utilities to cancel and I had to notify my landlord that I'd be moving.

About two weeks later I received a phone call from my friend Shannon, whom I'd met while I'd been working at Hahnemann University. We didn't talk often but always managed to catch up when we could. As I was going on about my move to Charlotte, I noticed she wasn't saying much. I assumed that she wasn't quite in support of my going away with Russell.

"What's up Shannon? You sound like something's bothering you."

"Well . . . " she hesitated, her voice soft, like she had a secret. "I have something to tell you Brenda, but don't know if I should."

"What is it? What's wrong?" I asked, now thinking something was going on with her.

She took a deep breath. "Remember how I told you that I'm friendly with Lynn, whose mom is friends with Russell's mom?"

"Yeah," I answered, confusing though it already sounded.

"Well, I called Lynn the other day, and when I asked if she was around, her mother told me—not knowing that I knew you—that Lynn had gone to Charlotte with Russell."

I gripped the phone, hoping it would keep me from falling. I felt a burning sensation in the pit of my stomach.

"Are you sure?" I murmured, hoping she wasn't.

"I am."

"How could that be? I don't understand. I mean, Shannon, why would he take her? It doesn't make sense."

"I don't know Brenda, and I didn't want to ask too many questions. But I knew how excited you were so I had to . . . "

I don't recall the rest of the conversation, other than wishing that I could scream over the mocking voices laughing in my head. It was not until I heard the insistent beeping of the phone that I realized she'd hung up.

I loosened my grip on the railing, moved down the steps and out the door. I needed air; the pain was stifling. I sat on the cement steps of my front porch wondering how I'd even dared to believe he'd changed. All those times I'd suspected it, all the rumors that he had other women, and the fact that he only stayed with me when he felt like it—now it was allin perspective and the sting of that reality was more than I could bear.

"Brenda, hey girl what are you doing over there?" my neighbor shouted from across the street.

Keeping Deborah in focus I made my way through rush

hour traffic on Lindley Avenue and blurted out to her what I'd been told.

There were no comforting words she could've said. I hadn't even known her that long. Instead she put her arm around me as the tears began to fall. When I'd exhausted myself I returned home and crept into bed hoping to escape my pain. I lay there thinking about how once again Russell had ruined things. I was determined to find out who this woman was who had pulled the rug out from under my feet.

In the morning my first call was to Selina, Tank's girlfriend. Tank was now serving time in jail for another series of bank robberies. According to Selina, nothing had been going on with Russell and Lynn prior to his trip to Charlotte. Supposedly she'd been having problems with an abusive boyfriend, and both her mother and Russell's mother agreed that since they already knew each other, it would be a perfect getaway for her.

I was well aware of Russell's reputation with women, and this trip was proving to be no different. My mind raced about what the two of them were doing down there together. The thought that another woman had enjoyed all the care I'd put into preparing him for that trip, the cooking, packing and senseless worrying, was making me crazy.

That evening when my parents dropped off Kelisha, I didn't dare tell them what I'd learned.

"So did Russell get on the road?" my father inquired.

"Yes. He called and said it's nice down there."

"I'm still not happy you're taking Kelisha away from us."

"I know, but it'll be good for the three of us. Just watch. Plus, Mom, it'll give you guys a place to vacation."

Always concerned about Kelisha, my father asked, "What if my granddaughter doesn't like it?"

"She'll be alright."

"And what about you?"

"Dad com'on I'm fine."

When they left, I went into 'mother mode' and focused my attention on my daughter. While I braided her hair we watched back-to-back episodes of *The Jeffersons,* then we read a bedtime story and I tucked her into bed.

I retreated to the living room, chain-smoked too many joints to count, and then called Lynn's brother Tony to find out more information. Tony was dating Russell's sister Ashley, who was in the hospital at the time with a chronic heart problem she'd suffered from since birth. Tony was even more knowledgeable because he and Russell had been hanging out a lot lately.

Using a fake name to get past his mother, I got Tony on the phone.

"Tony, its Brenda. What's with your sister Lynn and her going away with Russell?"

"Oh. Hey, listen, I can't talk right now."

"When can you talk?"

"I'll stop by tomorrow."

The following afternoon Tony showed up at my apartment. He gave me the same story as Selina, about how Russell wound up taking Lynn with him to Charlotte. Tony claimed that Russell had even left Bear behind at Eve's house. He said that his mother and Eve had practically forced Russell to take her, which pissed me off. Now I had further proof that Russell's mother was a troublemaking bitch who wanted me out of her life, and out of her son's life. Even more upsetting was the fact that Russell had agreed. I tried to understand why he'd deceived me. If it was just to help the girl out, then why hadn't he told me? Wasn't the reason for the move because *we* needed to get away? Well now he'd ruined our last chance and taken that time with someone else.

While Kelisha played outside with my Deborah's son, Tony and I sat in my kitchen drinking a six-pack of Colt 45 and smoking a joint. Getting high was the only way I knew how to squash the pain. Once Kelisha was asleep, I joined Tony in the living room where he did his best to convince me that Russell's decision to take his sister to Charlotte was no big deal. He insisted that he knew how much Russell loved me. That had never been a question in my mind; I was more concerned with the love he had for women in general. Tony might have been successful with his smooth talking if the

14

phone had not rang.

"Hey, what's up?" Russell asked, as if everything was normal, and he wasn't with another woman.

"Nothing much," I answered, waiting to tell him what I knew.

"Where's Kelisha?"

"She's sleeping."

I glanced across the room at Tony, who was sitting on the couch rolling a joint. A smug grin was smeared across his face.

"Listen, I need you to wire me some more money, alright?" he said, sure that I'd say yes.

I snarled into the phone. "Get it from that bitch you took down there with you!"

"What the fuck you talking about Brenda?"

"You know what the fuck I'm talking about! I'm sick of this shit!"

"Brenda who told you some shit—"

"Fuck you!" I screamed then slammed the phone down.

Tears rushed to my eyes. Even though Tony had witnessed my outburst and knew the reason, I still didn't want him to see me break down.

I left the living room with the excuse that I was going to check on Kelisha. I sat on the side of her bed, one hand patting her back, the other wiping my tears. What I really wanted to do was to crawl up in bed with her and pray that this had all been a dream.

A few moments later I heard Tony call my name. I returned to the living room.

"You okay?" he asked.

I plopped down onto the couch and cried to him about my love for Russell. He comforted me in his embrace while the phone rang incessantly. I knew it was Russell and didn't want to hear his lies.

To hell with him, I told myself. It was time for me to move on.

"So what you wanna do?" Tony whispered in my ear, catching me off guard.

Listless from the weed and confused about the fact that Russell was with another woman, I replied, "I don't care,"

Moments later I lay limp beneath a panting Tony. Somehow I'd convinced myself that I was getting revenge on Russell.

chapter two

A Scorned Man

There was a litany of phone calls between me and my girlfriends, discussing how I should handle the Russell situation. I'd spoken to his mother several times, but she claimed to not have known anything about Russell taking Lynn to Charlotte. Eve never knew anything if it was her son that was in the wrong.

Over the course of the week, I ignored my feelings and hung out with my friends. My time was spent at the bar on 5th Street or at my apartment partying with friends. Tony attended some of those parties, and eventually became a nuisance, begging to sleep with me again. I had no interest in him, and to make matters worse Selina even found out that a girl she knew from Russell's neighborhood was claiming to be pregnant with Russell's baby.

What brought everything to a boil, though, was a call from his sister Ashley.

"Brenda, its Ashley. I want to ask you something."

"What's that?"

"Did you sleep with Tony?"

I was shocked that she knew.

"What? What are you talking about? Are you crazy?"

"I don't think he would lie about something like that."

"Com'on you gotta be kidding me. Who told you that?" I asked.

"He told everyone you did."

"I really don't care what he said. He's a liar."

"I hope you know, Mom told Russell what Tony said and Russell's on his way home."

"I ain't worried because I didn't do anything," I replied.

"Alright, well I'm just letting you know."

Stricken with the reality that Russell would be coming straight to my apartment, I brought Kelisha back home, had my locks changed and decided it would be best if I shut down the partying. I tried to focus on who was really wrong here and felt certain that if he had not taken Lynn to Charlotte I would never have reacted by having sex with Tony. My friend Renée advised me that under no circumstances should I ever admit to anyone that I'd had sex with Tony.

The next evening, Russell's van pulled up and I heard him at the door attempting to use his key. Realizing that his key wasn't working, he began ringing the bell furiously and banging on the window. Scared of what he might do to the house if I didn't open the door, I went downstairs and unlocked it. I figured I was okay, because Selina was upstairs with Kelisha, and I'd already warned her to call the police if he got crazy.

"What the fuck is goin' on?" he asked, his face twisted and red with anger.

"Nothing," I replied haphazardly, blocking his entry.

He pushed me out of the way and stepped through the vestibule. Bear was jumping up on me, making paw prints on my white shorts and tube top. Russell unhooked the leash and the dog ran up the steps in front of us.

Kelisha stood at the top of the steps waiting for her father.

"Hi Dad!" she said. She was excited to see him, but he didn't have time. He leaned over, kissed her on the forehead and passed her by.

"Let's talk," he said, gesturing for me to follow him into Kelisha's bedroom.

I sat down on Kelisha's twin bed, my heart thumping so loudly I could hear it.

"What's up?"

He stood wide-legged in front of me and asked, "Did you fuck Tony?"

"No! Tony wanted me to, and he got pissed because I wouldn't give him any so he lied on me," I answered.

"I heard you and him spent the night together."

"That's bullshit Russell! Now why don't you tell me why you took that bitch to Charlotte with you?" I asked, hoping he'd see his fault in all this.

There was an audible SMACK when his open hand landed across my face. I grabbed my cheek to stop the stinging, praying that Selina would hear him and call the police.

While he walked over to lock the bedroom door I stood up, hoping to defend myself. I'd only made it easier for him to grip me around the neck with one hand and shove me into a corner.

He asked me again, "Did you fuck Tony?"

"I—I—" I stammered, gagging from the chokehold.

BAM! With his free hand balled into a fist, he punched me in my nose.

"Russell, wait please," I pleaded, throwing up my hands to cover my face. It was too late; his fists pummeled me until I was cowering in the corner.

"Git the fuck up bitch," he yelled, grabbing a handful of my braids and throwing me onto the bed. "You ain't nothin but a ho! How could you fuck my sister's boyfriend? *Everybody* told me you wasn't shit. As soon as something goes wrong you run out and fuck *somebody*."

Russell was always quoting "everybody" and "somebody" like those two words made up people who actually knew everything about me.

"What about you taking Lynn with you? How do you think I felt?"

"That ain't no reason for you to fuck my best friend."

Now Tony had become his best friend. It was pointless to even bother reasoning with him, let alone telling him the truth. He had already made up his mind that I had made an unforgivable error.

"You made me look like a fool to my family," he told me.

19

"What do you think *I* look like?" I screamed, hoping that the police would be arriving shortly.

Then it came.

CRACK! The blue nylon dog leash with "Chow-Chow" written on it whipped around my thighs.

"Russell, wait, wait, listen," I cried as I jumped up and down to get away from him.

He followed me like I was his prey, the dog leash whizzing through the air and tearing info the soft flesh of my skin.

I ran to the other side of the room, thinking I could hide in the closet. He only swung the leash higher, hitting me across my shoulders until I fell onto a pile of Kelisha's stuffed animals.

Determined to beat me into submission, Russell wrapped the leash tightly around his fist.

"You think you can just fuck over me, huh?"

I was crying too hard to answer, but nothing I said would've mattered. He was a madman and there was no reasoning with him.

He swung the leash high, and the metal clasp cracked against the bridge of my nose. Blood gushed out, splattering into my eyes and down my chin.

Bear's barking and jumping at the door must've made him regain some sense. He stepped back, looked at me and said, "Get up!"

Hysterically I cried as he led me into the bathroom. He closed the door behind us. I looked into the mirror, turned to him and asked, "Why did you have to beat me so bad?"

BAM! His closed fist cracked the left side of my temple. "You know the fuck why," he said. Then left me there.

I wished he had killed me. But that wasn't his style; Russell had perfected the act of torture. I looked into the mirror and had to cover my mouth to keep from screaming. I couldn't see where all the blood was coming from. I was sure I needed stitches to close the gash across my nose. I remained in the bathroom, wiping the tears and the blood until he banged on the door, ordering me to come out.

I discovered that Selina—rather than calling the police—

had left me there alone. My guess was that she didn't want to get involved, because Tank was her boyfriend, so she'd simply chosen their family over our friendship. Could I blame her?

When I came out of the bathroom, from the hallway I could hear Russell on the phone ordering a pizza. Kelisha sat on the living room floor watching television and combing her baby doll's hair. I didn't want her to see my mangled face, so I made busy in the kitchen. I'd found a band-aid in the cabinet that barely covered the cut on my nose, and I had to keep dabbing at the blood with a wet paper towel. Anytime my daughter approached me, I turned my head hoping to hide my face. Russell knew what I was doing and tried his best to keep us in separate rooms. Having no appetite, rather than eat I asked Russell if I could take a shower. But just as I was walking down the hall to the bathroom my daughter was coming out of her bedroom.

"Mommy what happened to your face?"

Even though I knew she sensed something was wrong, I had no idea how I could ever explain to my little girl that Daddy beat me.

"Nothing baby. I'm okay. I just fell in the kitchen."

By the time I'd finished in the bathroom, he'd put Kelisha to bed in her room and had pulled out the sofa bed for us. I wondered how he could look at my face and not feel bad about what he'd done.

"Brenda, I don't wanna hurt you. I love you," he said as he rolled a joint. "Don't you understand I was hurt because they told me you'd fucked that boy?"

He passed the joint to me. Rather than answer, I took a long drag.

"But Russell I didn't do it. You know I love you," I said, knowing what I'd have to do to get him to the other side of sanity.

Easing my head down between his legs he said, "Com'on then show me."

On my knees in front of him, my lips swollen from his beating, I took him in my mouth. I couldn't help but think that

21

maybe I was getting what I deserved.

We were sprawled across the bed, meshed in our act of sadistic lovemaking, when the phone rang. I was content to let it ring, but he lifted his head and said, "Answer the phone."

"Can I speak to Russell?" Tony asked.

My body tensed up. Why the hell was he calling here? What could he possibly want?

"He's asleep," I lied, not knowing Russell had been waiting for this call.

He snatched the phone from my hand.

"Yea, what's up? Did you fuck Brenda?" he asked Tony, now up on his feet, his eyes focused down on me.

I sat up in bed, scared of what Tony's answer would be. Would this man actually say yes, knowing the monster that resided inside of Russell?

"Stand up!" Russell commanded.

I did as I was told.

"Did you fuck Tony?"

"No Russ I . . . "

"Tony, did Brenda let you fuck her?" he growled into the phone.

Before I could duck, Russell's fist landed in the center of my face. Fresh blood oozed from the gash on my nose.

"Russell please, no. Don't—" I begged, using the curtains to protect my naked body as I fell backwards onto my many hanging plants.

He threw the phone across the room. For a while he just stood there watching me.

Gently, he put his arms under mine and lifted me onto the bed. "I'm sorry Brenda."

Sobs wracked my body until I felt Russell's lips on my neck and shoulders, making their way down between my breasts. I couldn't do this. I couldn't take the beatings and the lovemaking. It was driving me insane.

"Brenda, I really do want our shit to work out. Things are fucked up now but once we leave Philly they'll be okay. I want you to come back to Charlotte with me tomorrow."

"Alright," I mumbled. What else could I say? I would've

been a fool to tell him I hated him, because he would have beaten me again. It had always been my role in our screwed-up relationship to reassure him that I loved him and that I would never hurt him regardless of what he did to me.

I awoke the next morning wondering how I was going to get away from him. I knew he'd never let me out of his sight so I could make a phone call. When I looked in the mirror, it was as if I had two faces. Kelisha didn't ask any questions, because I'm sure she already knew better.

I went about my normal routine. I fixed breakfast for the two of them but couldn't eat, because the inside of my mouth was in shreds.

Since I'd agreed to go with him, he allowed me to walk down the street to the Laundromat. I pulled on a baseball cap and took Kelisha with me as he watched from the window. After finishing the clothes I walked back toward the apartment contemplating how to escape. As I approached the apartment I glanced up to the window. When I didn't see him I ran across the street to my neighbor's. Deborah answered the door, saw my battered face, and tears spilled from her eyes. I didn't have to tell her what happened.

I'd never let my family know that Russell hit me. Hell, if *I* didn't understand why I stayed with him, then surely my family wouldn't. I told myself that Russell and I had simply come from two different worlds; what was acceptable in his wasn't in mine. As a child he'd been exposed to violence, hunger, crime and unbalanced relationships. I, on the other hand, had been raised with family values, church on Sunday, and women who were respected. I'd never even witnessed my parents arguing. Of my five siblings—Joe, Gwennie, Gregory, Jeffery and me—I was the baby.

Deborah, though, convinced me that I needed my family. Using her phone, I called my brother Joe, and without giving him details, I asked if he'd come get me, because Russell was acting crazy and that I'd be on the porch waiting for him.

When my brother arrived, I was so overcome with embarrassment that rather than leave under his protection, I stayed inside. Watching from Deborah's bay window I saw my brother helplessly look up and down the street for a sign of me. Joe rang the bell of my apartment several times but Russell didn't answer. He then went to the phone booth and called, but I knew Russell wouldn't answer. Bewildered, my brother stood outside, yelling up to my apartment, desperate to know what had happened to his little sister.

After Joe left I phoned the police to have them put Russell out. When they arrived at Deborah's, they looked at me and said, "Miss, I'm sorry, but there's nothing we can do."

How could this be? Russell had beaten me with a dog leash, and they were telling me there was no recourse.

Deborah's phone rang. It was Russell. I took the phone and just listened to him apologizing, pleading and promising never to hit me again. I didn't believe him, because I'd heard it all before. He convinced me, though, to at least sit on the porch and talk with him.

His logic was to tell me how moving to Charlotte would change everything, how too many people in Philly were in our personal business. He said he didn't want to believe I'd had sex with somebody else, he didn't want Lynn, and that he loved me and wanted to leave tonight for Charlotte. I even asked him about the girl who claimed to be pregnant with his child, but he wasn't hearing any of it.

I wanted to believe him this time, to give him another chance to start over, so I agreed. When I went upstairs to pack, he called Ashley, who was now home from the hospital. She agreed to watch Kelisha for a week while I went with him to Charlotte. I would've preferred that my daughter stay with my parents, but that would mean they'd have to see my battered face. I knew, however, that if nothing else I had to call and reassure them that I was okay.

My father answered.

"Brenda, what the hell is going on? You called your brother over there and nobody answered the door. That boy didn't put his hands on you, did he?"

"No Dad, everything's alright. We had a little argument. It's no big deal. He didn't really hit me."

"Then why didn't you answer the door when Joe came?"

"I wasn't there. I was at the Laundromat."

"Well, where's my granddaughter?"

"She's here, but I called to tell you that I'm going to Charlotte with Russell tonight."

I could hear my mother in the background; I knew she didn't believe me. Nobody hated Russell more than Mary Thomas.

"Bring my granddaughter up here. Don't take her down North Carolina with that crazy man."

"Dad, tell Mom I'm leaving Kelisha at Eve's with Ashley, and we're only gonna be gone for a week, okay?"

"Bones, you know I don't like it." That was the nickname he'd made up for me since I'd always been so tall and skinny.

"I know Dad, but really I'm okay."

When we arrived at Eve's I didn't want to go in. I didn't want his family to see my face, but he insisted. Once inside the house they tried to act as if everything was normal, but it was obvious from the smirks on their faces that I looked like a fool. I was nauseated by the thought of putting my daughter in their care, but that's what Russell wanted. If that's what I needed to do to show him how much I wanted things to work out, I knew I had to do it. I kissed Kelisha goodbye, feeling sick inside because I knew she didn't like staying with them.

We spent most of the twelve-hour trip talking about our future. I was cautious in my conversation not to say anything that might provoke his anger. Russell was Mr. Happy-Go-Lucky, constantly reassuring me that the incidents with Tony and Lynn were in the past and that he'd never bring it up again. He certainly would never hit me again.

I was so emotionally exhausted and physically drained from his beating the night before that all I wanted to do was sleep. However, I didn't want Russell to think I didn't want to keep him company while he drove. I waited until he said it was okay before I lay down in the back of the van. As I drifted in and out of sleep I couldn't help but remember how this relationship had begun.

*　　*　　*

It had been March 1976 and I was 17 years old. I'd already known Russell Douglass probably 10 years, because his mother's sister, Ronnie was living with my brother Gregory.

Russell had recently moved into my neighborhood of Holmesburg and was living with my cousin Lena, with whom he had a 2-year old daughter, Toya. I wasn't certain what kind of relationship they had, because Russell was a ladies man and Lena was a "good girl" who always complained about his cheating ways and his often-abusive behavior. I couldn't see why she didn't leave him alone if things were that bad, but then again, what did I know, I was so young. How much did I really understand about relationships?

I did know that Russell had all of the things that made a man "fine." He was 21, a slender, 6'3" working man from West Philly. He had a light, smooth complexion and knew how to dress.

One afternoon I went to Brown schoolyard where the guys were shooting basketball.

"So, whatchadoing Friday night?" he'd asked when he came over to sit on the ledge beside me.

"Nothin', not unless you gonna take me out." I joked, noticing he even looked good when he was sweaty.

"Solid. Then meet me on Stanwood Street at nine o'clock," he said.

"Okay." I answered without thinking about the conesquences. I figured what the hell? We'd been friends, almost family; the most we'd probably do was smoke some weed, which was my favorite pastime.

My best friend Renée and I rarely did anything without consulting each other first. The great thing about being friends with her was that she was six years older, and much more experienced when it came to life. The one thing her experience hadn't taught her yet was how to get out of her abusive marriage to the father of her three sons.

When I confided in Renée that Russell and I were supposed to hook up she warned me against it.

"Don't do it. You'll get caught up like me, unable to get out," she'd said, referring to the fact that she was having an affair with my brother Gregory.

"Alright, then I'm not going," I said, actually believing that I wouldn't.

That Friday night as Renée and I were returning from *The Lounge*, the neighborhood bar where my cousin Lena was a barmaid, we spotted Russell's red 1966 Mustang turning the corner of Welsh Road and Erdrick Street. He pulled up to the curb and called me over.

"Where were you at? I thought you were supposed to meet me," he asked, smiling up at me from the window.

"I was on my way." I lied.

"Well get in."

I ignored Renée's advice, waved her on and slid in next to him. After riding around for a while, smoking joints and listening to music, we wound up "down by the river," a stretch of the Delaware that was located behind the Police and Fire Academies on State Road. At night couples would go there under the pretense of watching the "submarine races." Those races were a joke, of course, because what really happened was back-seat sex.

Still, I didn't think this first drive would lead to that. As he sat there comfortably swigging from a pint bottle of Jacquin's vodka, I couldn't understand why I was nervous. I'd been around him countless times, and he'd flirted with me plenty but it had never been just the two of us. My excuse for not showing any interest in him was that he had a baby with my cousin, which meant trouble if I crossed that line. But this kind of trouble felt exciting.

Getting relaxed from the vodka, I found myself babbling about nothing in particular. Without asking, Russell leaned over and filled my mouth with his tongue. The boys I'd gone to high school with—the ones on whom I'd wasted my virginity—had never kissed me like that.

"You better stop playing around," I said, nervous that he was serious.

He gave me no time to gather my thoughts.

"Why don't you get in the back seat?"

"It's too small back there," I said, hoping to deter him and myself.

Ignoring me, he climbed into the back seat and pushed the front seats forward. I took another sip of his cheap vodka and followed. Once we managed to get both of our long bodies situated, Russell started kissing me again, this time he used his hands to massage my small breasts while he entered me with a dick that was as golden and as long as he was. It was incredible.

After that night the passion between us became intoxicating, and we began confessing our love to each other. Sometimes we'd do simple things like going for long walks in the park, riding bikes along the trails in Pennypack Park, talking about what we wanted in life, our families and playing in the fall leaves that he knew I loved to crush with my bare feet.

He would take me places: movies, restaurants, or drives to Atlantic City. This was before there were casinos, and we'd just walk on the beach and stroll the boardwalk buying pizza and playing games to win stuffed animals. He also introduced me to a whirlwind of cheap motels and hotels up and down Roosevelt Boulevard. Most importantly he showed me life outside of Holmesburg, taking me out of my sheltered environment and exposing me to a world beyond my suburban zip code.

I had always wanted to escape the Northeast. There were very few Blacks among the mixed population of Caucasians, Jews and Italians. "The Bottom," where Russell was from, was situated between 34th and 46th Streets (Lancaster to Girard) in West Philadelphia. It was famous for its crime, poverty, and nightlife—something I only saw from the screen of my television. He'd grown up the oldest of five children raised by a single parent, his mother, with whom he got high. Adjusting from life in Holmesburg to hanging out in "The Bottom" was an eye-opening experience.

With all the time Russell and I spent together, it wasn't long before Lena discovered our secret. Russell's response was that she was the wrong woman for him, and it was me he really loved. My instinct was to understand his situation; I never thought of Lena's or even my own. It was easy for me to do that, because I'd lived among cheating men all my life.

My brothers and uncles were forever unfaithful, sometimes passing women back and forth to each other. I'd witnessed this behavior for years. So for a man to have more than one woman became acceptable. My parents always told me to take heed of my brother's womanizing ways. More importantly, they told me to never let a man use me. But at that time I still wasn't listening.

Unable to stomach our growing relationship, Lena decided to take Toya and visit our cousin in Los Angeles for a month. During her absence Russell easily convinced me to come to their apartment. I'd stop by on my way to the bakery in the morning, and I'd visit him late at night, each time we made love. He wanted me with him all the time, even when other people were there. Their apartment was the first place I cooked for him, or for any man. I took baths with him and went down on him; I did everything I'd ever read in *Cosmopolitan, The Sensuous Woman,* and any other publication that would help me show Russell that I was a woman. I'd even stopped writing my usual radical poems of the 70's and switched to poems professing my love for him.

The week before Lena returned, Russell told me he thought it would be best if we stopped seeing each other until he broke it off with her. He swore to me that he'd move out of the apartment, and then we could resume our relationship. I had no problem waiting. I loved him.

Lena came home and things grew ugly. All kinds of rumors were flying around about us—some true, some not. I secretly wished I could talk to Lena and separate some of the lies from the truth. It wasn't as if I didn't like my cousin. I actually envied her; she was older, beautiful and always had men flirting with her. I tried not to care about how I'd betrayed this woman who was my cousin, with whom I'd spent holidays, attended family barbecues. But none of it mattered, because my cousin was hurting and I was the cause. I buried any feelings I had of guilt, simply because I loved Russell.

Russell kept to his word, and within a month they moved apart. He moved to his mother's and Lena to her mother's— with me to blame for the split. I tried not to feel bad about it; I believed that it was meant to be this way. It wasn't my fault that Russell and I loved each other even though that love led to the emotional deterioration of my cousin.

One afternoon the inevitable happened. Renée and I ran into Lena outside *The Lounge*. We had the first of a series of confrontations.

"Brenda, you ain't shit. Why you trying to take my man?" she asked as she stood posted against a stop sign.

"Fuck you Lena. Ain't nobody trying to take your man!" I belted out the insult; I was trying not to look at her for fear that I would loose my nerve if I acknowledged my guilt.

"That's your fuckin' problem—you ain't no good. Why don't you get your own man and leave mine alone?"

"Russell was messing with a lot of women before I came along," I said, telling her what she already knew.

"Bullshit, Brenda, this is the second time. Don't forget Michael."

She was right; Michael Sheldon had been Lena's boyfriend while having chosen me to be his *other* girl. Our three-year relationship, even though sexless, had been one filled with passion and promises. It was Michael who'd taught me how to say "fuck it" so people wouldn't know how I felt, but he'd never told me the consequences of stuffing those feelings behind those words.

Being someone's other woman, although exciting, came with a big price. I was labeled the "bad girl" and that reputation had already destroyed a valuable friendship long before Lena.

Sharon Woodridge had been my best friend during the first three years we attended Lincoln High School. We shared all of our secrets and future plans. Unlike me, Sharon was a "good girl" who didn't get high, cut school or hang out with the wrong crowd. But we somehow balanced each other out— envious of each others personalities. It was during the height of our friendship that I betrayed Sharon, losing my virginity to her boyfriend, Bernie. It hadn't been something I planned, it was just that Bernie and I hung out in the same crowd and one night I got so high I wound up in the backseat of his car. Rather than chalk that one time up to a mistake I continued to see him.

Months later when Sharon got word that I was hanging out with her in the daytime and hanging out with Bernie at night she terminated our friendship. That friendship took us 30 years to rebuild. But between then and the time I began to see Russell all those feelings of guilt had been bottled up and now I had new ones to go along with it.

"Please, Lena. Maybe you need to learn how to keep a man." I bragged even though I had no idea what I was talking about.

She flipped me the finger and walked away.

Lena wasn't the only one coming down on me about my relationship with Russell. His family was now telling him how terrible I was, saying that if I could have sex with my cousin's man, then I'd probably sleep with his brothers, uncles, stepfather, whomever. I was surprised by their behavior, especially his mother's—I thought I'd bonded with her while getting high during our late-night talks. They'd been so accepting of me when Lena was in L.A., but now they'd all had a change of heart.

My family tried to tell me to leave him and his family alone, telling me they were trouble. It was too late; I was in love.

My mother was the more outspoken of the two and never held her tongue if she had something to say. Hell, once when she was mad at Russell for the all the havoc he was wreaking on our family, she'd beaten him with an umbrella! It was right after Lena had run into me and Russell outside of *Judy's Bar* on State Road. Lena chased us both until we jumped in the car and locked the door. When my parents found out about the incident, they were mad that I was not only making a fool of myself but embarrassing the Thomas family. So when my parents caught up with us that night at my brother Gregory's place in Whitehall Projects, my mother came in the house swinging her umbrella, and shocking the hell out of Russell.

My Dad, better known as Pop-Pop, was the more laid-back of the two. He rarely became excited about things. He always tried to reason and understand, but when he passed his limit, you knew hell was about to break loose. My parents were the only ones out of both of their families who managed to keep their marriage together, and for that, they were envied.La-La had five sisters and one brother, while Pop-Pop had two brothers and one sister.

At 17, I didn't understand why no one could see that Lena had been the wrong woman for Russell, that he'd made a mistake and it was me he loved. It was simple to me, but complicated to everyone else. They had no idea how he made me feel. It was like all the stories I'd read in magazines and books when I was younger. Love made you feel safe, comforted and happy; it made you want to be with that person all the time. I'd even read along the way that sometimes you didn't find love in the right place, but that if you hung in there, it would work out. That's what I was doing with Russell, hanging in there.

*   *   *

So laying there in the back of the van, my face battered and bruised, I realized I was still trying to prove to Russell that regardless of what I'd done in the past I was still good enough to be his woman.

chapter three

Sugar Creek
September, 1982

We arrived in North Carolina early the next morning and checked into a room at the Alamo Motel on Tryon Road. I met Russell's new friend, Sly, and we hung out, smoking joints and drinking beer. While giving us a tour of the darker side of Charlotte, Sly casually tied a rag around his upper arm in order to showcase a blue vein. He pricked himself nonchalantly with a heroin-filled needle. I didn't want to act surprised, but this was a first for me. I could never deny I enjoyed getting high, and since high school I'd tried many things, but watching him fade into a nod was quite unnerving. I thought that if this was what Charlotte had to offer on our first night, my expectations were already being cut short.

Our money ran low after three nights at the Alamo, so we parked in the driveway of Sly's parents' home, sleeping in the van at night and showering in the morning after they'd left for work. My time during the day was maddening—while Russell worked I was forced to sit in his hot-ass van all day reading novels and waiting for him to get off. My only relief from the scorching North Carolina heat was walking Bear or strolling through a mall to soak up the air conditioning.

After two weeks of living in the van we were approved to rent a small two-bedroom rancher with a yard. 3508 Spencer

Street was located off Sugar Creek Road and it was less than ten minutes from Russell's job.

The night we moved in, I was crampy—I had my period, I was moody and I hadn't had a shower in two days. Rather than stay there that night and sleep on the floor, the plan was for me to return to Philly by bus and pack up the apartment. So I hopped on a Greyhound and went home. Russell was to come get us the following weekend. By then my bruises had healed, so facing my parents—who'd picked Kelisha up from Eve's the day after we'd left—was not an issue.

Once I was back home Kelisha and I began packing up the apartment and waiting for Russell to call. A week later, when I hadn't heard from him, I decided to return to Charlotte. Louise and John, friends I'd worked with at Hahnemann University, drove Kelisha and me down along with the plants and clothes I'd crammed into their Volkswagen.

We arrived that afternoon and were greeted by our neighbor, Kat, and her 20-year-old son Buster, whom I'd met briefly before I'd gone back to Philly. They were more than eager to tell me how much fun they'd already had hanging out with Russell. On this day, however, he was nowhere to be found. Walking through the house I noticed he'd picked up a few things. The most interesting of which wasn't just the makeshift bed he'd created of a mattress and blankets, but the camera atop a tripod that faced it. I thought this was strange, because I knew the only purpose for setting it up like that was to take pictures of someone having sex. I put it out of my mind for the moment and focused on locating Russell.

Louise and John headed back to Philly later that night, leaving Kelisha and me alone in that house, waiting for Russell. I decorated the house with the few things I'd brought to give it a more homey feeling, but it didn't quite do the trick without any furniture. There was no clock; I had no watch and the radio shows were a far cry from WDAS-FM with Dr. Perry Johnson. As I attempted to entertain my daughter, I was missing home already.

Russell never did come home that night. The worst thing I imagined was that he was already spending time with another woman.

Early the next morning I heard his van pull up. I went to the door and watched as he twisted up his face, letting me know he wasn't happy to see me there.

"What you doin' here?" he asked, climbing out the van.

"I had to move out of the apartment and I didn't have anyplace else to go. Where you been all night, looking all worn out?" I asked cautiously.

"I went to Ocean City with Sly," he said, walking through the door.

Puzzled, I asked, "You went all the way to New Jersey over night?"

He picked up Kelisha as she came running from the bedroom.

"No, there's an Ocean City down here. Anyway how did you get here?"

"Louise and John brought me." I answered, not really believing his Ocean City story.

"I hope you brought some money."

"Of course." I responded, knowing that my having money would lighten his mood.

That week I enrolled Kelisha in kindergarten at Plaza Road Elementary School, which was two blocks from the house. I walked the neighborhood, familiarizing myself with the area. There was a Winn-Dixie grocery store, a liquor store and a Stop-and-Go. I liked the open, country feel, but we certainly weren't living on the better end of town. We were situated behind an industrial park, so there was more brown grass than green. Luckily for us and the neighbors, there was a community garden across the street that mainly consisted of turnips, which I'd later come to detest.

The one thing that it didn't take me long to recognize was that all my neighbors were drunks: the white couple who lived across the yard, the family that lived behind us and, of course, our neighbors who lived on the block. There were plenty of children, though. For that I was happy, because Kelisha would have playmates.

I learned from Kat that Russell had had women to the

house. One of them was a girl on our block, a mother of five children. Russell denied this, saying she'd shown him her southern hospitality by bringing him a plate of food. But as much as he tried, there was no denying the one that showed up at our front door. Rather than argue, I believed his lies and accepted it when he told me it was my fault for having left him alone for those two weeks.

At the end of September we made a weekend trip to Philly and back, packing up the remainder of our things fast enough that Russell wouldn't miss any time from work. This time, in addition to our furniture, clothes and, of course, Bear, we had the extra baggage of Russell's younger brother, Juan, his girlfriend and her son. It seemed they, too needed a new start, thanks to Juan's run-in with the police. Russell offered to let them sleep on the sofa bed until they got themselves together and found work and a place to live. I didn't question Russell's decision to bring them along, but I didn't quite understand how we could help anybody when we were barely standing on our own feet.

Even with me working temp jobs to help out with expenses, Russell had the burden of trying to support six people. I'd swallowed my pride and gone to the food bank to get some staples—milk, bread, cereal, butter and eggs—delivered to our house, but it just wasn't enough. So when there was absolutely no food and we tired of eating catfish stew complete with the heads that Kat offered, we took to other means: stealing our chicken and steak from Winn-Dixie.

One night in our desperation to get high, we drove to a place where they sold drugs, and when they brought it over to the van we snatched the 1/4-ounce of weed and sped away.

We didn't have a phone so Russell's mother would call next door to Kat's and talk to Russell about me, mostly telling him how much Ashley hated me because I'd slept with Tony. She was insistent that he and his brother return home, because his sister was getting sick. She would also tell him things I'd supposedly done, things I never even came close to doing. Anything she told him, he believed. Russell would accuse me of so many things that I often questioned myself, wondering if perhaps I'd forgotten something I'd done.

Finally he admitted to sleeping with Sandy, the young girl back in Philly who was pregnant, but he adamantly denied the baby being his. This I didn't believe. He kept trying to reassure me that it wasn't his, but his history with women caused me to have serious doubt.

The other pressure he was feeling was that Lena was relocating to Los Angeles with his daughter. I did my best to convince him to visit them before they left Philadelphia, but he refused to go.

One afternoon, while I stood in the kitchen cooking dinner, Russell strolled in from work. He had the mail, which included a letter from his brother, Tank. As he stood behind me reading, I felt the heat of his breath on my neck before he spoke. "Tank says he knows some shit about you."

"He don't know nothin' about me," I answered, as I continued to stir the simmering rice, wishing I had the nerve to pour it on him.

"My brother don't lie," he proclaimed.

"Who said his mouth was a prayer book?" I asked smartly, wondering if maybe Tank did know something about me. But how could he know anything? He'd been in jail for the past few years. He couldn't turn on me. I'd been one of his biggest supporters, having once been fool enough to get involved with one of his bank-robbing scams—a stunt that had had federal agents banging on my Lindley Avenue door.

Russell went into the bedroom. A few minutes later he told me to come in and close the door. I crossed the room and stood behind him, allowing me to see his reflection in the mirror. He sat deep in thought, his hands untwisting a wire clothes hanger.

"Take off your clothes," he told me, his head bent over, looking like a master who was about to discipline his slave for disobeying.

"Why Russell? I'm cooking dinner," I said gently, trying to get out of the room without angering him.

He cut his eyes at me, daring me not to obey. Out of fear I slid off my pants and unbuttoned my blouse, hoping that he just wanted to have sex. I would have readily submitted, but I knew I was about to submit to something far worse.

"Did you sleep with Tony?" he asked.

"No Russell. Why are you bringing that up?" I answered from behind him, still wearing my panties and bra.

"What does my brother know about you?"

"Nothing. I don't know what he's talking about."

"Did you fuck Salim, that guy you used to work with?"

"Hell no! Why do you always do this?" Salim was a friend of Tank's whom he'd wrongly accused me of sleeping with, as he did many of those in our circle.

Russell still hadn't turned around, but I could see his face had begun to turn red and tense as he gritted out the names of men that I'd been associated with but hadn't necessarily slept with.

"Yeah, well what about Malik? Shit you probably fucked Tank. How many men have you had?"

"Russell why are you doin' this?" I pleaded.

I watched tentatively as he straightened the hanger out into a long narrow rod, testing its strength by swatting it against the bed. I froze in place, unable to believe he was planning to whip me with that hanger. If he wasn't, then why else would he have it in his hand? How had he come to that?

"Brenda, tell me—why ain't you no fuckin' good?"

I was terrified, and my mind raced trying to figure out a way to get out of this.

"I am good, you—"

Russell rose from the bed, seemingly taller than he'd ever been. His movements were swift, and all I heard was the whiz of the hanger when it came down across my calves.

"Why you always fucking over me with other niggas?"

I tried to run from him, but he grabbed me with his left hand, twisting my arm behind me and slapping the wire down across my thighs.

"Russell, stop, stop—" I screamed, hoping my daughter wouldn't hear me but that his brother Juan would. He ignored my cries and kept bringing the hanger down across any part of my body that I couldn't hide with my hands.

"Bitch shut the fuck up and tell me why you always fucking over me?"

The searing sting of the hanger on my skin rippled throughout my entire body.

"Russell, please! Stop! I'm not—" I screamed.

"How come you can't be good like other women?" he asked while giving me another welt across my back.

I danced around the room trying to get away from his lethal weapon. "I swear I can be a good girl."

"Why you always making me look stupid to my family? When you gonna tell me the truth about Tony? How could you stoop so fuckin' low to fuck my sister's boyfriend?" he asked before planting another whack between my breasts.

Somehow I managed to get to the bed, where I covered my face with a pillow and balled my body into a knot. The room grew quiet and I hoped he was realizing how insane this had all become. When I peeked over the pillow he was unbuckling his pants.

"I need you to suck my dick."

I couldn't answer because the tears were coming too fast.

"You can stop that fuckin' crying."

He yanked the pillow away. "You want some more?"

He didn't wait for a response. He just grabbed me by the hair and pulled my head down between his legs. When I opened my mouth to receive him I wanted to make him feel the pain I was feeling, but I didn't have the nerve to sink my teeth into the soft flesh of his dick. Instead, I unenthusiastically sucked it, holding it in my mouth as he moved it around inside me.

"You better do it right before I fuck your ass up."

I obliged, realizing that once he came, he would leave me alone and feel bad the next morning for what he'd done. That was how it always was. When I submitted to him sexually it somehow made him feel like less of a beast. At that moment I didn't care. I just wanted the beating to stop.

He withdrew from inside my mouth. "Turn over."

I rolled onto my stomach, and he plunged his dick deep inside of me. He was gentle at first, and then his thrusts got harder until the pressure of his body against the welts on my back caused me to tell him how painful it was.

"Russell, you're hurting me," I murmured.

"I love you," he whispered in my ear, as if he really did. "I don't wanna hurt you. I don't want anybody else to have you Brenda."

I cried for the confusion. I really wanted to believe he loved me in his own way. But this sex act was sick, because Russell had the ability to beat me and make me want him at the same time. Maybe I was really the monster.

"Fuck me back!" he demanded when my body wouldn't respond to his.

"I can't," I mumbled, my head buried in the pillow.

He yanked my hair. "What the fuck did I say?"

I moved my body to his rhythm, praying that this act would soon be over. He put his lips close to my ear, his tongue licking me all over my neck and shoulders.

"You love it, don't you?"

"Yes," I whispered, scared to say anything else.

"You gonna let me stick it in your ass?" he asked, as if I had a choice.

"No Russell, I can't. Please."

"Why not?"

"It's gonna hurt."

I knew there was no rationalizing with him. He pleaded with me for a few minutes, and then realizing that I was denying him, his pleas turned to demands.

"I want some ass, and if you don't give it to me I'm going to take it!"

I cried harder, knowing I'd once again lost another battle over my body.

With one hand he spread my cheeks as he used the other to slather baby oil between my crack. He entered me slowly, causing excruciating pain. The dirty scent of sex and blood made it hard to swallow back the vomit that had risen in my throat. But what I couldn't swallow was the pain of my body being split in half. At that moment I vowed that one day I would kill Russell Douglass.

The next morning I awoke in debilitating pain, yet I went through the motions of fixing him breakfast and preparing Kelisha for school. As he left for work he asked for a kiss, as if there had been no night before.

After that episode I decided I would leave Russell and return to Philly. Of course, I couldn't tell him because he would have killed me.

Within a month I'd saved enough money from the temp jobs I was working to purchase two bus tickets.

I drove Russell to work one morning, and then headed downtown to the Greyhound bus terminal. I phoned his job and spoke to his boss.

"Hello Mr. Teller, this is Russell Douglass' wife," I said, always using the title that I didn't officially have because sometimes girlfriend just wasn't appropriate.

"Yeah Ms. Douglass, do you need your husband? He's in the middle of running a job right now."

There was no way I could give Russell the opportunity to change my mind. "No, no I don't want to speak to him. If you could just give him a message."

"Sure thing. What's that?"

"Tell him that he needs to get a ride home because I'm leaving his van at the Greyhound Bus Terminal."

"That's it? That's your message?"

"Yes, thank you."

Kelisha didn't know why we were leaving so she was excited about taking the bus home. Late that October night we arrived in Philly, my parents didn't ask any questions, because there were no visible bruises. I simply told them I'd left Russell because I couldn't take living with him and his brother. During the middle of the same night I'd arrived, however, Russell called and told my Dad he was on his way to Philly because he wanted to talk to me.

By 3:00 the next afternoon Russell had made the 10-hour trip from Charlotte and was calling me, begging and pleading for me to hear him out. As always I relented. I met him in the parking lot of 7-Eleven on Frankford Avenue, where we sat in the van talking.

"I know I was wrong. I fucked up, but you don't understand. We started out wrong. This time if you come back it'll all be different."

It was at these times when he would beg for me back that I was able to open up and say things that I couldn't say at other times, when he had me imprisoned between guilt and my next beating.

"Russell, you're lying. All you're going to do is act right until you get me where you want me, and then it'll be the same old shit. You're always bringing up the past. I never do that to you!" I screamed at him.

"Brenda, I swear I'll let that old shit go and I'm not gonna hit you anymore. I love you. You know it. You know me better than anybody. I thought you understood me."

"But what about your mother and your family? You know how they talk about me," I said, hoping he'd see what pressure they put on our relationship.

"Brenda, you come before my family. You know that."

His promises were nothing new. I'd heard them before, but he sounded sincere and I so badly wanted to believe that he really wasn't a bad guy. It was either that or the fact that as we sat there talking we were also filling our nostrils with cocaine—this always made his words sound more believable.

chapter four

Road Trips
Winter, 1982–1983

Upon our return to Charlotte, Russell kept all his promises; no arguments and no beatings, at least for a little while. Juan returned with us but without his girlfriend and baby. Russell allowed me to enroll Kelisha in ice skating lessons, which enabled us to get out of the house once a week. He even let me give Kelisha a birthday party. This of course turned into a party for our friends, at which he became so intoxicated that he began to take his clothes off and I had to put everyone out. Sadly, times like this were some of our more enjoyable moments, because I knew that if he was too high to think of himself, then he'd stay violence-free. As long as he wasn't beating on me I didn't care what he did.

Russell and Kelisha did well together but she was no "Daddy's little girl" like her mother had been. The only one who spoiled her was Pop-Pop, and he was too far away for now. She and Russell did have their fun, however. There were water fights, trips to the store and they'd play games outside.

For me, being pregnant with Kelisha had been my happiest times with Russell. It was also the only time period in which I didn't get high. But as much as Russell liked to believe he'd always been there for her, he wasn't. Hell, when our daughter was 10 months old I'd allowed a stranger to perform oral sex on me so I could get money to purchase Kelisha her first pair of hard-bottom shoes. It wasn't that Russell didn't have the money; it was just that he'd opted instead to buy his mother a blue fox fur coat.

The first time he ever became angry with Kelisha was one night when we were leaving the Eastland Mall. Russell had stolen a winter coat for her and we were outside in the parking lot when she asked him about it.

"Dad, did you steal that coat?"

He yelled at her, "Don't fuckin' worry about it. Just be glad you got a coat to wear."

I never feared that Russell would hit Kelisha but his harsh words were enough to frighten any child—especially one who'd witnessed his violent behavior. To comfort her I draped my arm around her shoulders and walked with her to the car. I'd like to believe that if he ever hit her I would've fulfilled my promise of taking his life.

"You alright?" I asked her quietly so Russell wouldn't hear as we got into the car.

She nodded yes.

"You know Daddy loves you, right?"

She didn't answer.

Unfortunately, this return to Charlotte was like all the other numerous trips we'd made up and down the road. It was far from a fresh start, because the getting high, the women, the lies, and his missing time from work were all the same. When I questioned myself as to why I stayed I just felt like there was no place for me to go. Russell had also done an excellent job of convincing me that I truly wasn't any good. There were things I was guilty of but none I thought were bad enough to bring on continuous punishment. At the same time, I always felt destined to be with him—like this was the life I deserved, even though I never knew what I'd done to deserve it. I believed that underneath all that anger and abuse was a good person only I could see.

When beating after beating began to wear on me, however, I got so tired of aching and feeling bad that deep in the recesses of my mind I allowed myself to dream about what it would be like to be on my own. I imagined Kelisha and me in our own apartment, doing mother-and-daughter things that didn't include her father. Believing that one day it would come to fruition, I tucked that dream away in my heart,

In the midst of it all, things starting looking up when I was blessed to land a six-month secretarial assignment with IBM. I told myself that at 25 years old, I was finally on my way to having a career. Being a secretary had never been a career goal of mine, just something I'd been good at. My mother had told me when I was in high school that as long as I could type I'd always be able to find a job. This was a funny thing coming from a full-time homemaker, but she was right. It was uncanny how savvy my mother was even though she'd lived a sheltered and protected life.

I'd had other career aspirations along the way as well. My first choice had been to be a lawyer, because I liked the attention they commanded in a courtroom. I'd also wanted to be model, maybe even the first black Miss America. I was certainly skinny enough, but when I asked my mother about going to modeling school she told me that models were nothing but whores. Maybe that wasn't so insightful, but I took her advice and left that idea alone.

But I became aware as early as elementary school that I wanted to be a writer. Once the teacher had asked what I wanted to do with my life and I'd proclaimed, "I want to write my autobiography." This, of course, was certainly long before I knew I'd have a life to support one. But that dream went deferred—if not by high school, then certainly after my encounter with that infamous Adidas sneaker.

My mother was no stranger to my writing. She, too, had found a journal that described intimate details of my lovemaking with Russell. Not only did I catch hell, but I was doubly embarrassed when she told my father what his baby had been doing. But she never judged. In fact, I took her silence as a secret encouragement.

Now in my mid-twenties, my dreams of the catwalk and the courtroom were behind me, and since I valued living too much to get caught writing even in secret—let alone for a living—I pursued being a secretary. Being a secretary at IBM allowed me to save money unnoticed by Russell. I told myself that I would use this savings to eventually move away from him. Surely North Carolina was big enough for the two of us.

Kat gladly provided me with information about Russell's trysts with other women, some of whom came to the house while I was at work, but she couldn't be trusted. I used this information as an incentive to keep me focused on my end goal of leaving him. According to Russell, it was she who was constantly making passes at him and never completely dressed when he'd go next door to use the phone. I didn't dare confront her about it because Kat was a southern woman who believed that people could be rooted under the spell of southern witchcraft. Instead I turned to my friend Tia.

Russell and I had begun hanging out with Tia and her boyfriend Milton and she was the closest thing I had to a friend. She had also witnessed Russell's abusive behavior and claimed to sympathize with me. What neither Milton nor I knew was she sympathized with Russell even more.

Our next visit to Philly was a difficult one. Russell's sister Ashley had died, and I was forced to go where I wasn't welcomed. The night we arrived at Eve's I tried to feel a part of their family but it wasn't working. Jena, Russell's other sister, was giving me dirty looks all night and making snide remarks about how I was no good. He in turn developed chest pains and shortness of breath so his mother gave him a Valium and made him go to bed.

Unable to go to my parents until morning, I sat downstairs getting high with Eve until Kelisha started nodding off to sleep. They didn't offer us a bed so I made one out of blankets on the dining room floor where we slept for the night.

I was always glad to go home, because it gave me time to spend with my family. Some of my happiest times were at my parents' house on Mill Street where there was always the smell of food, Pop-Pop in his recliner, and La-La being busy around the house. But the special times were when family would show up for the holidays, or just for Sunday dinners where my cousins, nieces, and nephews would all crowd into the dining talking trash.

To me, I had the perfect family growing up. We pitched pennies and played Monopoly; my brothers loved tickling me till I cried. I loved watching my brothers impersonating the Temptations. Being home with them was always revitalizing for me, even if I had to anguish over my return to Charlotte.

Once we were back in North Carolina, it was just the three of us. One of Russell's major points of harassment, however, was that I'd somehow contributed to the death of his sister. His family had told him that since I'd slept with Tony, Ashley had had a heart full of hatred, which added to her illness. I was amazed that he actually believed this and tried as I might to convince him otherwise, many nights he would torment me for hours because of this, ultimately forcing himself on me. Or maybe it wasn't force, because knowing that sex was the only thing that stopped him from kicking my ass, I offered myself to him willingly. But I wasn't just fighting Russell on those nights; it was Eve—she had always been, and would always be the voice inside his head, the voice that told him when he was young that he was a punk, a faggot and had meted out physical abuse to him and her other children.

An Oedipus Complex is what a mental health professional may have called the relationship between Russell and his mother, the woman who was the epitome of the strong, black woman, the woman he claimed to admire and love, yet feared.

The next visit was over the Christmas holidays, which I was glad to do since our Thanksgiving had been spent receiving a free meal at a local shelter in Charlotte. It was during this visit that I told my parents about my plan to move away from Russell. They were in agreement that it was good idea but thought it even a better one if I'd come back home.

This was the visit when Sandy delivered a little boy whom she named Russell J. Douglass. This birth gave Russell a bond with another woman that would last a lifetime; it also gave him a total of three children by three different women. I reminded myself that it had just been a few years ago that I'd had his baby while he was in a relationship with my cousin. I tried to tell myself there was a difference, but the only difference was

47

that I knew Russell had intended to get Sandy pregnant.

The birth of Russell's son also managed to tear the scab off an old wound. It was about a year before we'd moved to Charlotte and Russell had begged me to have another baby. I'd tried to give him what he wanted, but my body just wouldn't cooperate. In defeat he'd given up, telling me it was my fault I couldn't conceive. His words were, "if you can't have my son then someone else will." But that didn't bother me as much as his claiming it was my fault because I'd probably already killed his son.

What he was referring to was the abortion I'd had a few years prior.

*   *   *

It had been late in the summer of 1978 and I was 20 years old. We'd been living in our first apartment at 38th and Baring Streets in West Philly. Kelisha was about to turn a year old and my period was late. I made an appointment at the University of Pennsylvania clinic where they took a urine sample, examined me and told me I was pregnant. My immediate reaction was, "I can't have it. I'm not ready for another child." I was thinking of the harsh financial strain I was under and the lack of support I received from Russell.

The little Asian doctor responded with, "When you leave here go to the Short Procedures Unit on the third floor and they will take care of it for you."

I was in a daze as I walked to the third floor where the receptionist handed me brochures and asked, "Is this what you really want to do?"

"Yes, this is what I have to do," I answered, never considering that maybe I actually did have a choice.

She then scheduled me to have an abortion in one week.

That evening when Russell came home I told him I was pregnant.

"Well, you know what you gotta do, cause we can't afford no more kids," he'd said.

During the week Russell began to make comments about

keeping the baby, but every time I wanted to discuss it he would say, "You know what you gotta do." These responses made me unsure if he was toying with me or if subconsciously he, too, was undecided about our having anther child.

I didn't tell my family, just his mother who assured me that because of her own experience that having an abortion would be no big deal. I also confided in my friend Neicy, whose family had taken me in when Russell's would shut me out. She was the only friend I had during those early years when I lived with Russell at 38th and Baring Streets.

The night before the procedure Russell promised to come directly home from work so he could go with me. I waited for him as long as I could, but he didn't show. So I took Kelisha to day care. I then returned to the apartment to see if he'd arrived home yet, but he still wasn't there. I knew he was messing around with a young girl from Holmesburg who he was dropping off at high school on his way home from work in the morning. He'd already found someone younger to replace me. Figuring this, and knowing there wasn't much I could do about it, I left him a note and walked to the hospital. It was a long walk down 38th Street and over to 34th and Spruce, which gave me ample time to change my mind. I knew it was wrong to kill my baby, but I didn't have anything to offer another child—I was barely able to provide for Kelisha without my parents' help.

I arrived at the hospital mixed up from all my thoughts— by the tears streaking down my face it was evident to the intake nurse that I was on the verge of an emotional breakdown.

"Is this what you really want to do?" she asked, trying to console me.

"I'm doing what I have to do." It was the only response I could offer between my outbursts of tears.

"Try to calm down. Maybe you'll feel better when you get around the other women. Is anybody here with you?"

"No."

I returned to the waiting area and watched the other women sitting with their husbands and boyfriends and wondered why

Russell couldn't be there for me. At the same time, what I also realized was that he was never there for me; I was only there for him.

The nurse came out and called three names, one of which was mine. I stood up and followed her into the locker room. I couldn't stop crying, so she pulled me aside and asked me if I was sure this was what I wanted to do.

"Yes," I mumbled.

We undressed and the other women tried to comfort me, telling me that it would be okay. One woman even bragged about how this was her fourth time, which made me feel worse. I couldn't imagine how any woman could repeat this process and not learn anything from it the first time. The nurse returned and told us to follow her. She put us in separate beds, and I lay there thinking about how God was going to punish me for what I was about to do. At one point they warned me that if I didn't calm down they wouldn't perform the abortion. I thought if only Russell were there to tell me that I didn't have to go through with it . . . before long it was my turn.

They wheeled me into a small white operating room. It was very bright and everything looked sterile and shiny. The doctor stood at the end of the gurney dressed in green scrubs, and explained to me how he would proceed.

The assisting nurse placed a steel gray bucket in front of the doctor who then positioned it in between my legs. Was that where they would place the pieces of my baby? I tried not to get hysterical, but it burned my throat to hold the tears back. I was injected with a local anesthetic and given another needle to relax me, but nothing helped with my excruciating emotional pain. Once I was numb, the doctor used a tube with a suction cup on it—an apparatus that resembled a vacuum cleaner—to begin pulling pieces of my baby from my womb. I could feel him sucking my life out of me. I wanted to think clearly to tell them it was hurting, that I didn't want them to take my baby, but I couldn't get through the numbness or the drugs.

Within a half hour the procedure was complete. Since the medicine hadn't totally knocked me out, when they wheeled me back into the recovery room I became hysterical. The nurses couldn't control me and threatened to put me in restraints. All I asked for was the picture of my daughter out of my locker. I wanted to look at Kelisha in case God decided to take her from me for the act I'd just committed.

Two hours later the nurse told me I was being released. I sat up and tried to pull myself together. I managed to get my clothes on; all the while I was hoping Russell would be in the waiting room when I came out. He wasn't. I walked home, slower this time because I was weak and cramping. When I arrived at the apartment Russell wasn't there but he'd left a note, which read, "Why did you kill my baby?"

I was devastated; how could he be so heartless? More importantly, how could *I* have been so stupid? At the time I never even considered the fact that I could've made my own decision, that it was my body to make choices about.

I called Eve to see if he'd gone to her house and when I told her about his note she casually told me, "Don't worry, it's no big deal."

I went to the refrigerator—the only things we had to eat were Chips Ahoy and Cool Whip. On the mattress, on the floor, in the living room, I sat, dipping the cookies into the cool whip until it was time to pick up Kelisha.

Russell came home later that evening and we argued. He told me how he cried when he'd come home and realized what I'd done. He kept asking me why I did it, and I told him because he told me I had to. He began calling me a murderer. I didn't know what to say; I didn't have the strength to argue with him. For weeks he tormented me about it, telling me I'd probably killed his son. All I could do was smoke one joint after another to block out the sting of his words.

*   *   *

Five years later, in January of 1982, another woman—with whom he'd only had a fling—was able to give him what he wanted.

chapter five

Friday the 13th
May, 1983

It was clear after a short time that this entire move to North Carolina had been a disaster. There was no starting over for us, and I was a fool to think that there ever could be.

By the end of April, Russell was fired from his job for missing too much time from work. We then woke up one morning to discover that his Dodge van had been repossessed—supposedly they'd tracked him down through his money order payments, which still hadn't equaled out to what he owed. He called Eve, and she insinuated that I had probably called the bank on him. I pleaded with Russell and explained that I wouldn't do that, because I used it to get to work everyday, but he didn't care. If his mother was making the suggestion, then it had to be real.

With all the eviction notices we'd received for non-payment of rent, I didn't want to be caught off guard so I began to put my plan in place. The money in my envelope at work had grown to $1,000. I went looking for apartments, and eventually I was approved for one on the other side of Charlotte.

I knew I'd done the right thing when I received a phone call at work from my neighbor.

"You better come home. You gittin' set out," Kat said in her country drawl. She'd warned us that in North Carolina, if you didn't pay your rent you could be forcibly evicted.

"What?" I asked, puzzled as to what she was telling me.

"They setting your stuff outside."

I called for a cab and told my manager I had to leave for a family emergency.

When the driver turned onto Spencer Street, I saw my neighbors huddled in Kat's yard. There were three police cars and officers blocking the path to my yard. Trudging back and forth were two bulky men whose job it was to remove our belongings from the house. Pictures, dishes, clothes, furniture, everything and anything we owned had been stacked in the yard. Even our family pictures had been put back on top of the television.

"What the hell is going on? What are you doing with my stuff?" I shouted to the sheriff while throwing money behind me at the cab driver.

"Ma'am you can't go inside."

"Why not? It's my house! You can't do this!"

"Ma'am I'm sorry, but we can't let you in. You're in the process of being set out for nonpayment of rent," he told me, glancing down at the eviction notice.

"This is my fuckin' house," I said, as I attempted to walk around the skinny sheriff.

I called over to Kat, "Where's Russell?"

"He ran off when the sheriff showed up."

What kind of man was he, leaving me to handle this alone? I looked at my watch—it was 2:00 p.m. In an hour Kelisha would be coming home from school. What was I going to do? What would I tell her, that she had parents who could no longer provide a roof over her head? Maybe, I thought, this was working out for the best. My parents were coming to visit in another week; if I could hide out in a hotel until then, they could help me move into my apartment. In the immediate, though, I had to protect my things. I couldn't let my daughter be embarrassed *and* scared that she was alone.

I pleaded with the sheriff.

"Listen, I got to get in my house, this ain't right."

"You're gonna have to calm down ma'am," he yelled at

me.

"Ain't nobody calming down! Why couldn't you wait?" I asked boldly, my face in the sheriff's as I watched the men carry out Kelisha's overflowing toy box.

"Ma'am in that case, is this here your drug paraphernalia?" he asked, pointing to the bong, pipe, seeds, roaches and marijuana plants that sat on the coffee table in the front yard.

"I don't want to hear about no damn drugs. I want to get in my house. Now move!"

"That's it. We're locking you up for possession of the paraphernalia," he said, leading me by the elbow towards the police car. He handcuffed me and sat me in the back.

I didn't think the sheriff was going to really lock me up – maybe just let me cool out until the movers were finished. I was wrong; they had every intention of doing their job and drove me down to the Mecklenburg County Jail.

At the jail I was directed to sit on a bench in the receiving room until they called my name. They asked for all of my vital information, but I had no address to give them. They sent me to talk to a counselor who asked me how long I had lived in Charlotte. Since it hadn't been a year, and I had no place to live, according to North Carolina law, he couldn't release me on my own recognizance. He did offer the number of a bail bondsman who could assist in my posting bail.

I called the bondsman and gave him the proper infor-mation. Of course, he needed a reference and of course, cash. Next was the hard part—phoning my parents.

"Mom, is Daddy there?"

"Yeah Brenda, what's wrong?"

"Nothing. You're still coming this weekend aren't you?" I asked imagining the two of them sitting at the dining room table, coffee cups before them and me about to cause a rise in their blood pressure.

"Of course. I already started packing," La-La answered, always happy to be going on a road trip.

"Okay, well, I need to speak to Daddy."

"Here, Thurmond, your baby wants you."

"What's going on Bones?"

"Dad, I didn't want to tell Mommy, but we got set out today."

"What do you mean? You moved already?"

"No. We got evicted."

"Kizzy, where is she?" Dad asked, using the name he'd given his granddaughter because she'd been born during the year of the *Roots* mini-series.

"Kiz is still at school."

"Well where's that damn Russell?"

"I don't know, but Dad that's not the problem. I'm in jail. I sort of got locked up."

"For what, Bones?"

I went on to tell him about the paraphernalia and how the bail bondsmen needed them as a reference in order for me be released.

"Give me the number. I'll take care of it."

Up until this time the police hadn't put me in a cell. As a matter of fact, they were being quite nice to me. I thought that meant I was exceptional, that I didn't belong there because I hadn't committed a real crime. Then they changed shifts and one of the guards decided that I needed to go into a cell.

A woman officer escorted me, along with two other female prisoners, upstairs to the second floor. One at a time the guard told us to undress and take a shower. I did as I was told and stepped into the dirty, green stall where it was safe to cry. I showered with no soap. When I finished she proceeded to spray me with insecticide in every spot that I had hair.

I kept trying to tell her that the bondsman was coming for me and that I wasn't going to be there long.

"Yeah, that's what they all say," she said, laughing. Then she handed me a pair of asparagus-green pants and a matching shirt to put on. She opened the door to another room, which was a large cell shared by a number of Hispanic, Caucasian and Black women.

Inside the cell there was about 20 cots, arranged bunk-bed style across one side of the room, where women sat in the beds reading letters and books. On the other side there was a warped brown picnic table that held a 15" black-and-white television. Across from the table was a makeshift bathroom. It was only a toilet and sink with a shower curtain pulled around it.

I sat at the picnic table for the better part of an hour, until a guard opened the door and called my name. Once back in the hallway, she handed me my clothes and told me to get dressed. I did as I was told and followed her back into the elevator.

She led me to a visiting room, where a screen separated me from the bail bondsman. I explained the story to him, and he said he would have me released within the hour. I remained in the visiting room until he completed his paperwork, and then I was able to walk out of the door, to where my friend Tia was waiting for me, having received a phone call from Kat.

I had a million questions for her, the first one being 'where was Russell?' She said he'd found an apartment and was moving our stuff in. I couldn't imagine how he'd accomplished that. She told me Kelisha was safe at Kat's house. This all complicated my plan to leave Russell.

The next thing I wanted to do was get something to calm my nerves. Tia handed me a fresh joint, which I smoked in between gulps from a 16-ounce can of Old English.

When we arrived at Kat's my daughter ran up to me.

"Mom what's going on? How come I can't go home?"

"You remember I told you we were gonna move?"

"But where's all my stuff, and where's Daddy?"

"I don't know yet but everything is gonna be fine. Mommy has a place for us to live, okay?"

"But I want to go home," she wined.

I smoothed out her hair, unable to tell my daughter that we no longer had a home.

Finally, Russell called Kat's house, excited that he'd found a place for us to live. He even thought it was funny, my having been in jail. It seemed he'd applied for a townhouse in a community that was about 10 miles from where we lived. Instead of waiting until Monday for approval he only waited for the office to close, then he and Milton moved our things into an empty unit that was minus hot water and electricity. I couldn't believe it—we were now squatters. What was my life coming to?

That night we bathed at Kat's sister's house. Luckily, Kelisha was able to stay with them. I later walked up the dirt road to the convenience store, where there was a phone booth, and called my parents. I told them where I was and that I was okay. I brought a bottle of Tiger Rose wine and returned to the house. After Tia and Milton left, Russell and I went to bed, set up in the living room which we had lit with a few candles. Making love that night felt dirty as we lay in a strange house among filth, not far from a bathroom that wasn't even fit for use.

The next day, Friday, May 13, I called my parents. They said they were still coming on Monday. I was happy to hear that, because I knew that I would be leaving Russell and starting a new life with just Kelisha and me. I was having second thoughts, though—maybe moving to the other side of Charlotte would not be far enough. What I really wanted was to take my daughter and go home.

We started getting high early that afternoon when Tia and Milton arrived. Tia was due to return her father's car, making it the perfect opportunity for me and Kelisha to get a break. We went to the park first, smoked a few joints, and talked about my leaving Russell and how outraged he was going to be. I made her swear once again that when I left she wouldn't tell him where I lived.

Later that evening Russell and Milton began calling Tia's house, wanting to know when we were coming back. We told them we no longer had access to the car and that they should find a way to come get us. They claimed they'd been taking speed pills (or "speckled birds", as they were commonly referred to) and drinking Thunderbird. Russell said he didn't want to leave the house unlocked with our stuff inside.

I'd known for a while that Tia's parents didn't like me, and it became more obvious when they came home that night— they clearly didn't want me and Kelisha spending the night. I wasn't sure why they felt that way, because I'd always been respectful. I assumed it had to do with the fact that Russell and I were from up North and our ways were too fast for their southern-raised daughter. But I'd learned one thing on my own about southern women and that was that they were far from slow—especially when it came to men.

Tia, however, convinced her parents to let her borrow their car to take me and Kelisha back to Kat's. I think they agreed because they were happy to see me go.

I was getting Kelisha ready for bed when Tia called, saying frantically that Milton and Russell had kicked in her front door. Her parents had called the cops and Russell was in a cab on his way to Kat's. I knew what was next.

"Kat, listen—you gotta call the cops before he gets here!"

"I ain't got to call no cops. This my house and Russell ain't gittin' in!"

"You don't understand, Russell is crazy. You can't stop him when he gets like this."

"You go on in the back with your daughter. Imma handle this."

"Please Kat, please call the cops!" I begged her.

I sent Kelisha to Kat's bedroom to sit with Lainie, her teenage niece, and I waited with Kat for the nightmare to begin.

BAM, BAM, BAM! Russell's fist pounded on the front door.

"Russell you git on away from here," Kat told him.

BAM! "OPEN THE FUCKIN' DOOR BRENDA!" he yelled above the noise of his foot kicking against the plywood panel.

"Russell you get on away from here!" Kat hollered back.

"OPEN THE DOOR KAT! I WANT TO TALK TO BRENDA."

"I ain't opening no door cause you high Russell."

"I'm gonna kick it in if you don't open it."

I pleaded. "Russell please go away, we can talk tomorrow when you calm down."

THUD! THUD! His body slammed against the door. I could see the hinges tearing from the frame. He was coming through.

The two of us ran for cover in Kat's bedroom. We dragged Kat's dresser across the door to barricade ourselves inside.

After one more series of ramming, Russell was in the house. Then, like a wolf in sheep's clothing, he knocked faintly at the bedroom door, trying to fool us into thinking he'd calmed down.

"Brenda, com'on talk to me *pleeease*."

When he pushed against the door and it wouldn't open, he yelled. "LET ME THE FUCK IN!"

"I'm calling the cops Russell," Kat said, then she told her niece to do so.

But I knew it was too late, he was too close.

My daughter sat hugging herself on the floor next to the TV stand. I patted her on the head, "Kiz, everything's gonna be alright, Daddy's just acting a little crazy."

"I'm scared Mommy. I wanna go home."

"Don't be scared, Mommy isn't going to let anybody hurt you," I said, not being so sure that was true.

"Brenda come help me hold this door!" Kat demanded.

When I went to help her, I could see that Russell had managed to get his arm through the door. Kat was jabbing at it with a pair of scissors. She had pierced his skin a few times, but it only infuriated him more.

BANG! BANG! BANG! The door toppled onto the two of us. I fell backwards onto the bed, and Kat ran to the other side of the room.

Russell leaped on top of me, a sledgehammer raised above his head.

"Brenda, what the fuck is wrong with you? All I wanna do is talk to you," he tried to say calmly through his drug-induced stupor.

Before I could respond to him, the sledgehammer came crashing down against my left shoulder. I heard a snap, and a fire-like sensation shot across my chest.

My voice exploded. "RUSSELL, YOU'RE GONNA KILL ME!"

"Brenda, I wanna talk that's all."

"Okay, okay—please just let me get up," I said.

My body squirmed beneath him, but not quickly enough. He swung the hammer again, grazing the back of my head.

"Please talk to me, I don't want you to leave me, Brenda," he cried, holding onto me.

"Stop hittin' me Russell, and I'll talk to you," I said, my voice full of pain.

He scooped me up in his arms as Kelisha watched, her pretty little face covered in fear. I managed to pull away from him only to collapse in the hallway, hoping that if I pretended to faint he'd leave me there. Instead he leaned over, grabbed me by the arm and began dragging me down the hall. Looking up into his face, his eyes glaring back at me I could see he could not be reasoned with. I stood on my feet and went with him out the gaping hole that was once the front door.

Once outside Russell dragged me through the yard, past our empty house, to where, I had no idea. I heard police sirens in the distance behind me but nobody was in sight, because it was at least midnight. When we got to the corner of Anderson Street, he pushed me into a yard and propped me against a tree.

"Brenda, I love you. Why do you wanna leave me?" he asked, kissing me all over my face.

"I'm not leaving you." I lied, realizing that Tia must've told him my plans.

He reared back, grabbed me by the throat with one hand, and punched me in the face with the other. "What the fuck is wrong with you Brenda? Why are you fucked up?"

"Russell, please stop. Wait, you don't understand. I wasn't leaving you, I love you."

He brought me to him, holding me so tightly I could barely breathe from the pain in my shoulder.

"Brenda, I'm sorry. I wanna talk to you," he whispered in my ear, his hands brushing through my hair.

"Okay Russell, we can talk, but something is wrong with my shoulder," I said, the piercing pain having made its way down my back.

He slapped me and said, "No it isn't, you fuckin' don't want me!"

The lights went on in someone's house behind us, so he grabbed my hand and led me across the street and behind a hedge of bushes. Roughly, his hands made their way between my legs as he tried to push me to the ground. He wanted to have sex with me, and there was nothing I could do about it. I stood in his arms sobbing until I noticed a police car turning the corner. I made a move to try to break from his grip, but he'd seen them too and held on to me tighter.

"See? I knew you were trying to leave me. Why Brenda? I don't wanna hurt you."

Once the police passed he sat me on a swing in the yard.

"Russell, where we gonna go? We have no money and no home."

"Don't worry; tell me you'll go with me."

"Of course I'll go with you, but you gotta stop hitting me."

"Brenda, I love you."

The police circled the block again, and this time I managed to make a run for the street. Russell ran out after me but the police car stopped. The cop jumped out, grabbed Russell and handcuffed him to the door. I stood shaking in the street, unable to even tell the officer my name while he phoned for backup.

An ambulance arrived and began treating me; I don't even think they knew what for. I was a mess—blood was everywhere. Once they had me on a stretcher, I glanced over and watched them load a crying Russell into the police van.

"Brenda, I'm sorry. I swear I love you."

They took me to Mercy Hospital, where after being examined by the doctor, I was told that I had a broken collarbone that would require a brace, and a cut in my head that needed stitches.

Fearing that he would come into the hospital after me, I refused to be left alone. The doctor kept telling me I was safe, but I didn't believe anyone when it came to Russell. Nobody could ever keep him away from me. The nurse then came into the room and told me I had a phone call, I asked her who it was and she told me, "Russell Douglass."

"Please, please keep him away from me!" I screamed, refusing to speak to him.

After a few hours I was released. But where was I going?

And how would I get there? I called Tia, but her parents wouldn't let me speak to her. I called Kat, but she had no transportation. I told her I had money in my jacket and that I would call a cab if she'd let me come back to her house. She agreed.

I took a cab to Kat's, where I found her house in shambles. I myself looked like something out of a horror movie: a bandage wrapped around my head, a brace around my shoulders and various cuts and bruises on my face. Kelisha, who was kept there safe by Kat, refused to come near me.

"Kelisha, come here to Mommy," I said, needing her more than she needed me.

She didn't respond and instead stepped backwards away from me while shaking her head no.

"Kelisha don't be scared," I said, seeing the fright in her eyes.

She shook her head no again and disappeared into the bedroom.

"I love you Kelisha. I promise Mommy isn't going to let anything happen to you."

"Let that girl be," Kat said.

Kat had already called my parents, but I called them again to let them know I was okay.

"Brenda what the hell is going on down there? Kat said Russell tried to kill you."

"I'm going to be alright."

"Not as long as you're down there. We're leaving in the morning to bring you home, you hear me?"

"Yes, Dad."

"Here—your mother wants to talk to you."

I could hear the fear in my mother's voice as she asked to speak to Kelisha. I told her she was asleep. I had put them through so much, and now this. I didn't know what to say to her. I knew I was ripping their hearts apart. All these years I'd tried to hide my lifestyle, and now it was out in the open. Realizing this, I knew I'd finally have to be honest with them about what had been going on in my life. It was somewhat of a relief, but I still had the night to go through, and Russell could always come back.

Eve called and wanted to talk to me. I took the phone and listened to her plead for Russell as she had done numerous times in the past; often it resulted in me taking him back.

"Brenda, are you okay? I heard what happened," she stated, faking concern for me.

"I'm alright," I mumbled.

"I know what happened, but Russell was really high. I know he didn't mean to do it. He told me that he'd taken some speed pills and was drinking. He said you left him."

"I didn't leave him," I answered.

"Well he's outta jail, and he doesn't have any place to go."

"So what do you want me to do?"

She paused, then asked, "Do you think you could give him a few dollars to help him find somewhere to stay? Right now he's walking the streets."

I was ready for her to be manipulative, so I stood firm and simply told her I couldn't help him.

What I didn't dare tell her was that there was an unhealthy part of me that wanted to see him, wanted to hear him beg for forgiveness. I wanted him to kiss me, to tell me he would make it up to me and, of course, then he would make love to me. That would make everything better. It was all part of the twisted relationship that had somehow managed to consume me. What was wrong with me? I didn't know how I'd turned onto this path, and that scared me—because I didn't think I could get off.

My parents arrived the following day, and I had no choice but to face them. When their car pulled up in front of Kat's house, Kelisha ran out to meet them as I stood timidly in the doorway.

"Jesus Bones, what happened? Look at you—that boy is crazy."

"Where's my—" my mother began to ask after Kelisha, who whizzed by me and into La-La's arms.

"Mom, Dad, this is Kat."

"Hey Mr. & Mrs. Thomas. You daughter's gonna be alright but that Russell, he's crazy."

"I can see that. He practically killed you," La-La said,

looking at me pitifully.

"This here is the door he broke down," Kat told them of the awkwardly repaired front door and the bedroom door that still lay in the hallway.

They didn't stay long at Kat's. It was bad enough seeing me, but the damage to her house compounded it. Plus, she felt the need to keep rehashing the story. I guess she was processing it all too. My parents didn't want to even try to put in perspective what had happened, let alone subject Kelisha to reliving it. Apparently they had anticipated the worst, because they'd already rented a room once they'd gotten off I-85.

La-La, Pop-Pop, Kelisha and I checked into the Days Inn on Sugar Creek Road and stayed until I went to court for the paraphernalia charges.

Since I had the brace on and was in a lot of pain, my mother had to help me bathe. It was humiliating for me, and I'm sure she felt helpless seeing her daughter in such a state. I would listen to my parents on the phone, begging my brothers, cousins and uncles not to have Russell killed. My mother believed that Russell would eventually get what he deserved, and she didn't want any of them to be part of it.

For the next two weeks, I continued to go to work. I told my co-workers I'd been in a car accident. Eventually I told my manager the truth; she, in turn, shared with me that since my performance at IBM had been so positive thus far, she would refer me as a transfer to the Philadelphia office. This would get me out of Charlotte and away from the memories of horrible life I'd lived there.

I was cleared of the paraphernalia charges and told by the judge not to return to Charlotte, North Carolina. The night before we left the Sixers swept the Lakers and won the NBA championship, which gave me an excuse to sit at the hotel bar and get drunk.

I found out through Kat that Eve had wired Russell money, which he used to buy a car. He had returned to Philly where he would stay until he had to appear in court for the assault and battery charges.

Even though I told everyone I'd had enough of Russell

Douglass, deep inside I wasn't quite sure I had.

chapter six

Tainted Love
Spring, 1984

Now that I was back in Philly, people looked at me like the fool I surely was. I'd been back in town for only two months before I started getting messages that Russell wanted to see me and Kelisha. I didn't want to deny him his daughter but I had to admit I was also curious as to what he would say to me, how he would make it up to me, because I felt I deserved that much. My weakness for him, combined with my weakness for snorting cocaine, laid the path for my return. Within a month I was sneaking around to see him. I denied it to my parents until my Uncle Richard (my father's younger brother) ran into us one night at a restaurant.

"What the hell is wrong with you?" my mother asked one Saturday morning while we sat around the dining room table having coffee.

"Nothing."

"You must be sick or something to still see that boy after what he did to you."

"It wasn't like that Mom. He was on drugs that night."

"I don't give a damn what he was! He tried to kill you and now you sneaking around the damn streets seeing him."

I couldn't say anything because I had no recourse.

My father interjected. "I'm telling you right now—you can

make a fool of yourself if you want to, but I don't want that nigga calling here or coming to this house."

"Okay, okay, he won't."

I hadn't admitted it to anyone but I was embarrassed that I'd taken him back—that I had no consideration for my parents' or my daughters feelings nor what I'd put them through. Not only did I not have an explanation for them, but I didn't have one for myself.

At the time this was going on, my sister Gwennie was working for Women in Transition, an organization in Philadelphia that assisted abused women. Her experience with Women in Transition enabled her to easily see that I needed more than a shoulder to cry on.

I loved my only sister—she was often my guiding light. I had such fond memories of her as a child. She was so beautiful, and I enjoyed watching her take such pride in her appearance. Every bit of makeup had to be applied precisely. She would spend hours in the one tiny bathroom we had, which would drive my brothers crazy. I recall her making jewelry with little charms that spelled out the wearer's name, and those gum-wrapper chains she made out of Doublemint and Juicy Fruit wrappers.

When Gwennie was 12 and I was only two she fell and broke her hip, causing her to need surgery and spend most of her teenage years in a wheelchair. But that wheelchair never stopped us from going on family vacations: Atlantic City (a.k.a. Chicken-Bone Beach) every summer, New York City to the Statue of Liberty, down the country to visit my mother's family in Powhatan, Virginia. Gwennie left home when I was 10 years old and eloped with a man who had promised her the world and gave her nothing but struggle.

That summer my sister suggested to my parents that I get counseling. I appeased them by agreeing to go for a few sessions. My counselor, Sue, was a sister and I really liked her.

I visited her once a week and we had in depth conversations about my family and my relationship with Russell. I was stunned though when she asked, "Have you ever been with Russell when you weren't high?"

I had no idea what she was getting at. I'd been getting high since high school, where smoking joints had eventually led me to harder drugs—I'd once even swallowed a handful of children's Bayer aspirins to get high.

As for Russell, who I'd been with for 7 years, well not getting high had never occurred to me. It was part of who we were. That's what had drawn me to him, and I assumed it was part of the glue that kept us together.

During my therapy, a local talk show, *People Are Talking,* did a segment on abused women, and Sue asked me if I would participate. I agreed and when asked if I wanted to be on camera or behind a screen, I chose to be on camera. Instead of being embarrassed I felt proud that I'd been chosen to be on television and wanted the world to see me. Where was my pride?

They pre-interviewed me for the show, and since I was still wearing my collarbone brace I was the perfect candidate. The night before I was to go on, I spent with Russell. During the show the next day, I explained to the audience what happened to me in Charlotte, never mentioning that I was still involved with my abuser. I had no idea how foolish I looked and didn't even care. I wanted to be on television—it was almost as if I was boasting about what happened.

It was during this time that I first saw Rusty, Russell's son, who by now was about seven months old. Kelisha had been spending time with Russell at Eve's and would return home telling me how much fun Rusty was. One morning while leaving my sister's apartment, Eve was parked outside with Rusty in the car. Realizing he was innocent in this whole thing, I went over to see him. When she took him out of the car, he kept smiling at me with his little yellow face and hat cocked to the side, winning me over, like his father.

Russell asked that I spend some time with the two of them. It was his belief that Sandy was incapable of taking care of her son the way I could. I wasn't sure if that were true, or if he knew that would take away some of my insecurities. Eve thought it was great that Rusty could have me as a mother figure, which made me think I might get in her good graces.

69

What I didn't realize was that having Rusty also filled a void in my life. He took the place of the child I'd aborted. This, I thought, might keep him from running around on me. It seems crazy in retrospect that after he broke my collarbone with a sledgehammer and got me and my daughter evicted that I would continue to seek the approval of Russell and his family. Ineeded it, though. I needed that acceptance and felt like I could win it by being a mother to Rusty.

I finally heard from IBM's office at 17th and Market Streets and was hired as a word processor. Russell was also working and he'd gotten an apartment at 55th and Market Streets on top of a candy store. It was a pretty raggedy place, and we nicknamed it "no-light Dwight's"; the building's electricity kept getting cut off because the landlord, Dwight, wasn't paying the bill. So Kizzy and I would stay there Friday through Sundays, along with Rusty, who had taken to staying at Eve's. It was here that I truly bonded with Rusty, and without realizing it he was turning into my little boy. I potty-trained him and took him off the bottle, treating him as if I'd carried him in my womb. He repaid that love by calling me mommy. We soon became a happy family.

Kiz never questioned where Rusty had come from or how he'd become part of our unit. She'd been told that he was her brother and enjoyed having him there.

Even though we had made strides as a family, we still continued our drug use. Russell then began dealing cocaine—mostly to feed our growing habit. And along with his sister, Jena, we learned the art of freebasing, which was cooking the "cut" off the cocaine and smoking what was left. Some nights Russell would get so paranoid he'd have me call the paramedics to see if they could slow down his rapid beating heart. It's not wonder they didn't call the police to lock us up.

One Sunday while Kelisha and I were at Easter dinner at my Aunt Bootsie's house in Southwest Philly—a dinner to which Russell was not invited—we received the news that Marvin Gaye had been shot by his father. When I got home that night Russell and I began to discuss Marvin's music and his violent death which led to a conversation about the violence in our own relationship.

"Brenda I never really wanted to hurt you all those times. It was always the drugs, not really me," he said, as he sat there snorting lines of coke through a twenty dollar bill.

"I know you're not a bad person, Russell. I'm just glad its over and that you never killed me, because you'd be in jail and the children wouldn't have a father."

"You're right but—" he began to say before drifting off into thought.

"What?" I asked, wondering if he was having a moment of remorse.

"I don't know. It's not important."

"No tell me," I said, probably wishing I hadn't—it was him this time who reminded me of one of those moments I'd chosen to forget.

*   *   *

It had been 1981 when Russell told me he'd found someone else and was in love. So, in turn, I tried to find someone else. I'd met a brother on the subway who was fine by all definition: 6'4", teasingly tan, his head slightly balding. With Kelisha at my parents for the weekend I'd invited him over to my apartment on Lindley Avenue. We sat in the living room getting to know each other when a horn began to beep outside. I pretended not to hear it.

"Is that horn for you?" my date asked.

Brushing my plants aside, I looked out the window, and there sat Russell in his van.

"It's my daughter's father stopping by," I casually answered.

I walked down the steps to the door, pulled the curtain back looking at him, looking at me, owning me. Unlocking the door, I said, "I have company."

"So what?" he replied, as he ran up the steps two at a time.

Sitting there with the two of them made my stomach start to churn, and I needed to use the bathroom, but I didn't want to leave Russell alone with my date. The three of us sat there uncomfortably for all of twenty minutes. Finally, my date decided to leave. I took his coat out of the closet and walked him downstairs.

"I'm sorry," was all I could say, as he was never to be heard from again.

Russell decided he was spending the night. Once undressed he began fondling me roughly. I knew I wouldn't be able to stop him, but I didn't want to fight so I lay there with him on top of me, giving him what he came for.

"Suck my dick," he said, like he expected it.

"No Russell," I answered, annoyed that he had spoiled my night.

Surprised at my denial, he asked, "Why not?"

"Because you're out there fucking around with too many bitches!"

"You won't suck my dick but you'll hang up that nigga's coat? You don't even hang my coat up!"

"Russell, please don't start," I said, wanting to laugh at the irrelevance.

I noticed him reaching towards the floor into his pile of clothes where he shocked me by pulling out a .38 revolver.

"Russell what are you doing?"

He positioned the gun in his hand with the steel grazing my forehead. "If you don't suck it I'm gonna blow your fuckin' head off, Brenda."

"No . . . I'm . . . not sucking—"

"Brenda you're gonna do it or Imma kill your ass."

As he cocked back the trigger my body stiffened. With tears running down the side of my face into my ears I tried to reason with him, but he wasn't listening.

"Why are you doing this?"

My eyes followed his finger as it squeezed tighter on the trigger. Why, I asked myself didn't I just do what he wanted? Maybe I thought if he killed me I wouldn't have to suffer his beatings anymore.

Then it came; the hard butt of the gun hit the left side of my head with a force that made me think I had been shot. Blood gushed from my head, dripping down into the corner of my mouth, mixing with the tears and snot that ran from my nose. I heard him calling my name but I couldn't respond—I felt myself fading away—maybe I was finally dying.

"Now suck it!"

"I'm bleeding Russell, please—"

He reared back on his knees, leaned forward and shoved his dick deep into the back of my throat. "I don't give a fuck, suck it anyway!"

I sucked it with as much effort as I could before I started choking on my own blood and saliva. When he'd had enough he turned me onto my stomach and took me, violently, like he hated me.

"Come on, get up," he said when he'd finished.

He led me into the bathroom where after wetting a wash-cloth with warm water he stooped down and patted the blood away from my face.

"Brenda, I love you, I didn't mean to hurt you. I don't want anyone to have you."

I sat there hating the smell and touch of him, yet I knew that this was the part of him I loved: the part of him that was gentle and felt bad for the angry person he'd become. What I didn't understand was why he often had to almost kill me in order to express his love to me and want to touch me gently and with compassion.

I always thought it ironic that during that same year Russell, was the one who'd been shot. The same woman he professed to be so was in love with set him up to be robbed because he was dumping her after he'd received a cash settlement from a lawsuit. I guess it's true that when you play with guns they often backfire.

chapter seven

Solid as a Rock
1984–1985

After our dog, Bear, bit the landlord, Russell moved from "no-light Dwight's" and I went with him. We made our new home at Park Terrace apartments in Chester, Pa. My parents had no more energy to fight my decision to be with a man who beat me, but they did object to my taking Kelisha with me. I didn't fully trust Russell's new behavior either, so my daughter wound up being a weekend visitor.

Russell was laid off from work and receiving unemployment, which had become a habit of his—he'd work for a while and then be laid off. Our method was to use what money we did have to buy drugs and sell them, using the cash to buy more drugs and pay bills. This strategy never worked in our favor, because we were our own best customers, causing our drug use to reach new new heights. We were dealing and using copious amounts of a variety of substances. Either people came down from Philly or we picked up new friends in Chester. We were known as "the good-time couple."

Living so far from the city, however, and not having a car, crippled us. Russell purchased a yellow 1978 Capri four speed. Kelisha hated riding with me because I wasn't able to maneuver the stick with ease and we were always rolling backwards. That car lasted a good two months, which was about all we lasted in Chester. Our excuse was that the apartment had two many roaches but the reality was that we were unable to manage our money and our rent became delinquent.

My old neighborhood of Holmesburg was where we rented a first floor, two-bedroom apartment just two blocks away from my parents on Erdrick Street. Holmesburg was a close-knit community with about five streets of African-Americans. Its cornerstone, Mt. Zion Baptist Church, stood like a beacon on the corner of Erdrick Street and Welsh Roads. Like any small community, everybody knew everybody's business.

There'd been Sunday School picnics and Vacation Bible School, church activities, all the things that provided a safe foundation that I'd chosen to shatter. However, now I was hoping to bring that stability into my children's lives.

But it was also where'd I'd come into drugs. They'd come gradually; first there was smoking weed in the 9th grade because I wanted to be part of the crowd. I progressed so that by the 12th grade I was fully engrossed, taking speed, downers, and dropping acid. Snorting cocaine was expensive then, so we usually snorted monster so needless to say Russell and I had lot in common when we hooked up, because he'd been doing the same thing.

My parents were definitely glad I'd returned to the neighborhood; it meant they could keep their eyes on me. For me it meant Kelisha could live with us and still attend Brown School, where all her cousins went. At the time, however, Rusty's mother, Sandy, had her second child and was going through her own turmoil, so he was living with us full time. It was Eve though with whom I found myself in a constant battle, whether it was over Russell or Rusty she needed to control both. But Sandy fooled both of us and in a few months took Rusty to live with her in Ohio.

Having made the decision to move back to the city, using my IBM discount I surprised Russell by renting us a Cadillac for the Thanksgiving holidays. What I didn't know was that Russell had a surprise, too. We'd pulled up to my parents' house when he leaned over and said, "Here."

When I looked down he was opening a blue velvet box that

held a beautiful marquis-cut diamond engagement ring. I couldn't believe it; he wanted to marry me. I hugged and kissed him while the children jumped up and down in the back seat. Russell sat there smiling, satisfied that he'd finally given me something to be proud of. I ran in the house and showed my mother, who appeared to be excited, but I'm sure she realized more than I did how much deeper I was being woven into Russell's web. All I could think about was how I wanted to scream out to all of the women he'd ever been with that I was finally going to be Mrs. Brenda Douglass.

We settled into the neighborhood and quickly established ourselves as the go-to drug dealers and our business tripled. The first to benefit were the children. For Christmas there was the collection of Cabbage Patch dolls and a computer for 8-year-old Kelisha. For 2-year-old Rusty there was a shiny new bike, a drum set and expensive remote control cars that were too advanced for his age. We even made sure we sent boxes of toys and clothes to California for Toya, Russell's daughter with Lena, on her birthday and Christmas.

For ourselves, we shopped for fur and leather coats, diamond jewelry, Gucci purses and stereo equipment. We even purchased new gray leather furniture and glass tables for our apartment. But most of all there were parties for whatever reason we could conjure up. Whether it was a party to paint the apartment or celebrating that Bear had won a fight with another dog. And there were visitors day and night.

Drug use became a family affair. Ria, my 17-year-old cousin became useful for many reasons. She was our babysitter, housekeeper and she sold drugs for us at Lincoln High, the school she attended. My brother Gregory was also selling drugs and would come by every Friday night to cut and bag his coke. Some nights on my way home from work I'd promise myself that I wouldn't indulge but I'd always give in—even when I was sick.

To outsiders, and even to us, our life seemed decadent. There was always plenty of money which we could use to buy drugs. Russell was back to working the 4:00-midnight shift at Precise Grinding on Roosevelt Blvd, so I rarely went to bed before 3:00 a.m. We made it our goal to always have the best, whether it be whole filet mignon sliced to order, fresh lobster tails that Russell would bring home and cook in the wok, or Dom Perignon for our Mimosas.

Before heading to work in the mornings I would take vitamins with a cup of herbal tea and honey and roll a joint laced with coke to smoke while I got dressed. At work things were no different. If I was tired from being up all night I would go to the ladies' room and snort coke. At lunch I would walk the back streets and smoke a joint with my co-workers. Then there were always my favorite restaurants where I could eat lunch over a few drinks—Jimmy Milan's on 18th Street or Hedgeman's at 13th and Arch Streets.

My co-workers served as my personal customers; at lunchtime I'd ride with Rick to 8th and Butler Streets in North Philly to pick up small quantities of coke. When we worked overtime, Angel and I would lay our lines of coke inside our desk drawers to be snorted at our leisure. Then there were Cindy and Mark; they thought the art of selling and using drugs was something worth accomplishing. Mark, a branch manager, called me into his office one morning and slid an ounce of coke across the desk for me to sell for them.

Despite our 'high' times, the fear of Russell hitting me again came to fruition one night when I found myself being dragged by the hair from the kitchen to the bedroom. I can't even remember the reason why. When we'd fight I'd always try to muffle the sounds so the children wouldn't hear. Our arguments were usually about drugs and money or his being paranoid that I was cheating on him. Cheating was impossible for me to even consider, because I was too scared of him to take that chance, and surely not with anyone we knew. The accusations, I later found out, were a cover up for what he was doing.

My parents began to express their concern about our lifestyle and how it was affecting Kelisha and Rusty. They wanted to know why we always had a house full of people and why there was always someone knocking at our door. My Uncle Leroy and his wife Gladys lived next door and provided them with a full report of who came and went. I told them that whatever they heard were just rumors. For their benefit I began attending church at Mt. Zion with the children, where they sang on the youth day choir and went to Sunday School.

February 16, 1985 was the date we set for our wedding. It was hard for me to believe that at 28 years old I was getting married. I kept praying that Russell wouldn't change his mind.

I never prepared myself by thinking about what marriage meant or what the vows stood for, and pre-marital counseling wasn't even a consideration. I did suggest that Russell tell Toya that he would be marrying someone other than her mother, but he chose to let her find out on her own.

We'd planned to get married at Mt. Zion and to have Rev. R.J. Waller, Sr. perform the ceremony. I went with a 7:00 p.m. candlelight service even though we wouldn't be using candles. Renée would be my maid of honor, and Juan would be Russell's best man. The children would also walk as the flower girl and ring bearer, and my father would be giving me away.

Rather than a wedding gown I opted for a dress that I purchased from J.C. Penney in the Gallery. It was cream, with sheer sleeves, a lace bodice and a veil.

That evening as I dressed in my bedroom at my parent's house I was filled with nervous energy. Renée noticed my anxiety and offered me two #5 Valium before we left for the church. And when I entered the church and saw a handsome Russell at the top of the aisle waiting for me I couldn't have been more relaxed. Here was a man that everyone, including me, thought would never change. I thought that today proved to everyone that regardless of our past, Russell was taking me for his wife and it made me happy.

Kelisha went down the aisle first, followed by Rusty. It was a good thing he wasn't carrying the real ring, because he took off down the aisle and jumped into his grandfather's lap. What I wasn't sure of was why we'd allowed him to carry a plastic gun down with him. Next was Renée, dressed in a beige suit and matching hat. Finally, my Dad took my arm and proceeded to walk me down the aisle to my future husband. I can't imagine how that must've felt for my father, giving his baby away to a man who beat her. But since returning from North Carolina I hadn't dared complain to my parents about any violence in my relationship. They, too, must've thought it was over.

After the ceremony my brother Gregory drove us around in his two-tone, 1979 Bill Blass Lincoln Continental. The reception followed at my parents' home, where my friend Louise had made a beautifully decorated wedding cake, my aunts prepared the food and my Dad brought the liquor. The bride and groom provided the cocaine.

IBM had given me a week off with pay, but we hadn't planned for a honeymoon. Instead, at the last minute we used my Dad's American Express card to check into the Hilton on Civic Center Boulevard.

The next few hours of our impromptu honeymoon were spent sitting at the hotel-room table in our sexy nightwear ordering bottles of champagne. We added to that several joints and long lines of cocaine. By the time we were ready to consummate our marriage we were both wasted. Clumsily, we made our way to the bed and Russell slipped my nightgown over my head. When my stomach began to flip I thought maybe it was from all the excitement—until I tasted vomit in the back of my throat. I pushed Russell off me and ran to the bathroom, but before I could get there I was throwing up all over the room, leaving a trail to the toilet. Russell put me in the shower and called housekeeping to have them clean up the mess. It was a sure sign of things to come.

About two months after we were married, Laney, my manager, approached me with an opportunity to work on an assignment in Miami. The event was the 'IBM Means Service' awards, where IBMers who'd won an award for outstanding performance were acknowledged. The assignment would last for three weeks with plenty of overtime and doubletime. She suggested I check with Russell and see what he thought, since we'd recently gotten married. I told her to count me in and said I would confirm it the next day. When I told Russell he encouraged me to go—he saw it as a chance to make money both through work and selling coke while I was down there. At the same time, however, he kept bitching that he couldn't believe his wife (which he loved calling me) would be leaving him so soon after we'd gotten married.

In late April I left for Miami. I stayed at the Fontainebleau Hotel where all the activities were to be held. Our workload consisted of everything from administrative support to playing hostess at various events. We worked in shifts with plenty of free time to enjoy the festivities. They told us it was a privilege to work these events, and their motto was, "Whatever you see here, stays here."

On the night of the main banquet, my role was to play hostess. Following dinner the Temptations and the Four Tops entertained us. When the Temptations scanned the audience for someone to join them on stage, they chose me since I was sitting in the front row in a bright fuchsia slip dress. Once on stage I wound up singing "My Girl" with them. It was such a high for me.

My trip to Miami never included any plans to cheat on my husband, but when you mix coke and the Miami heat, things take on a life of their own.

One evening I began hanging out with a sexy Cuban man I'd met in the hotel bar. He showed me around town and took me to different clubs while feeding me coke in between drinks. It only seemed natural when I allowed him to return to my room. His attempt to have sex with me would've been laughable, except he made up for his lack of length and width with his tongue skills. That Cuban went down on me for the next hour without coming up for air. It was fine with me because I didn't have to return the favor. Before leaving he tried his best to convince me to go to Havana with him, promising me all the cocaine I'd ever want. For once, however, I didn't let my greed for a good time and endless supply of coke take over. I declined his offer and showed him to the door.

Needless to say, I fell in love with Miami; it was the ultimate place to mix business with cocaine. Russell and I had shipped enough coke and money back and forth via FedEx to land me in jail for quite some time. At the end of the three weeks I never gave a second thought to the fact that I'd cheated on my husband; it just seemed a part of my lifestyle.

A month after my return from Miami I'd taken a one-week vacation from work because my friends were telling me I needed to keep an eye on what was going on in my home. There were just too many young girls in and out when I wasn't there, under the guise of buying weed. Being at home allowed me to witness something that would stay in my mind forever—the Move bombing.

It was May 13th. I was familiar with the Move organization from the time I'd spent in 1978 living at 38th and Baring Streets, just a few blocks from their compound in Powelton Village. At the time Frank Rizzo was Mayor of the city, and since the neighbors complained that their 'back-to-nature' lifestyle and hatred of the police had become a nuisance to the community, he'd decided to create a blockade around their property. After several weeks the siege resulted in citations and confrontations, and a gunfight which left a police offer dead and several officers and Move members injured.

Now it was 1985 and with W. Wilson Goode as Philadelphia's first African American mayor, the battle with Move began with the group living in a house at 62nd and Osage Avenues. The police became so frustrated by their inability to chase Move members from the property that they literally dropped a bomb filled with C-4 plastic explosives on the house. I was mortified and unable to believe that a horror I only imagined could happen in the likes of some place like Vietnam, had taken place in my own city. It frightened me that those in power viewed this as a viable option to solve conflict. The bomb killed six adults and five children. That memory has never left me.

chapter eight

Disney World
Summer–October 1986

From out of nowhere Russell began to talk about getting the three of his children together. It could have been his desire not to repeat the pattern of his own father's behavior when he left his mother with three children. Whatever the reason he was determined for us to be a family. During those moments when we'd talk about the possibilities, I could see that he was interested in the benefits of family togetherness, and of course I wanted to be that strong woman behind him.

In my head I believed I was already focused on my children, but most times my head was somewhere else. One afternoon Kelisha came in the apartment from school complaining that her arm was hurting from a fall she'd taken at the playground. She insisted that her arm was broken but I ignored her cries and told her it was probably just sprained. It wasn't until three days later that I took her to Nazareth Hospital where after an x-ray the doctor diagnosed her with a broken arm. Then there was the morning I was turning the corner onto Mill Street, when Kelisha fell backwards out of the car. Fortunately she wasn't hurt, which enabled me to brush it off as an accident rather than poor judgment on my part. It never occurred to me that had I not been smoking weed laced with coke that maybe I would've checked to make sure my daughter was properly buckled and the door locked. I still didn't notice my lack of parenting skills when she cut her leg on a beer bottle while taking out the trash after a birthday party for Russell. Rather than checking to see if she needed stitches, I covered it was a band-aid because I was too busy partying.

The hardest part of our campaign to be good parents was Lena's refusal to cooperate—there was no way she wanted me in her daughter's life. We sought legal counsel from Jettie Newkirk, a custody lawyer, to determine if Russell could get partial custody or at least visitation rights, because the only time he got to see Toya was when he went to visit her in Los Angeles.

The lawyer advised us that until they went to court neither Lena nor Russell had custody of Toya. So Russell and I devised a plan to force Lena to Philadelphia so a custody hearing could ensue. We knew it was a selfish act, snatching Toya from Lena, but we felt it was our only choice.

Russell flew to Los Angeles on a Thursday morning and checked into a motel. He visited with Toya and Lena for most of the weekend, taking Toya back to the hotel with him at night. On Saturday afternoon, when Lena went to pick them up for the day, she discovered that not only had he checked out but also they were on a flight to Philadelphia.

Being unsure of how soon her family might show up on our doorstep, when Russell and Toya arrived I'd already checked us into the Quality Inn at 22nd and Spring Garden Streets. According to our lawyer we'd need to keep her in our custody until the papers had been filed. Since we didn't have any clothes for Toya we took the children shopping and to the hair salon. We went to the movies and out to dinner and even took the children to the "Please Touch" Museum. Our mini vacation ended when we returned to our apartment and Lena showed up with the police.

"Why'd you steal my daughter, Russell?"

"She ain't just your daughter, I got the right to see her too."

"I don't want her around that no good bitch. And you ain't no kind of father anyway."

"I can do better for her then you can. I don't know why you took her to California anyway. All her family is right here."

"What do you care? You was down North Carolina with *her*," Lena said pointing towards the open door.

It was heartbreaking to see my cousin standing there at the bottom of the steps and Russell at the top arguing over who was the better parent. I stayed inside the apartment so not to heighten the situation. But I heard my name mentioned numerous times. I didn't dare tell anyone about my feelings, but it was as if I had not only "taken" Lena's man but now I'd also "taken" her daughter. I felt so much remorse for all the pain I'd caused Lena, but nobody would believe me because I'd never let it show.

Toya sat and eavesdropped as well, until she became distraught and Kelisha informed us that she'd tied herself to the bedpost.

"I'm taking my daughter with me."

"That's bullshit. She's staying right here with me until we go to court."

The police officers voice cut through their argument.

"Sir. Ma'am. It doesn't matter who she stays with because Ms. Thomas will be unable to return the child to California until there is a hearing. So what do you say you let the child go with her mother Sir?"

I'm sure Russell saw that he'd hurt Toya more than he'd imagined, and that she really couldn't return to LA without going to court, so he relented and allowed Toya to go with her mother.

Two weeks later we were inside Family Court at 1801 Vine Street. The hallway outside of the courtroom resembled a circus. There was Lena's mother, her sister and a few friends whose evil glances weren't directed toward Russell, but came my way instead. I could hear them replacing my name with "that bitch." I pretended to ignore them but felt at fault for inflicting pain on my cousin yet again.

Tagging along with Russell and me was Eve, who always managed to play both sides of the fence when it came to Lena and me.

After the judge met with Russell and Lena, he called the family members into the courtroom to tell us that we had nothing to do with the matter. The judge had granted them joint custody, which consisted of Toya being with Russell for two months in the summer and on alternate holidays. Russell was also required to pay $50 a week in child support. I then reminded my husband to request that Toya be allowed to travel with us to Disney World in October, and much to Lena's dismay the judge agreed.

The seven-day Disney trip was something we'd been planning to celebrate Kelisha's upcoming birthday. The money we'd saved for the trip had been dipped into several times because of our lifestyle and we didn't want to forfeit our trip so Russell came up with an idea. He sat the children down and explained to them that if they wanted to go to Disney we had to sell drugs to get the money. The kids, in turn, offered to help by counting bags of joints and stacks of money, leaving the cocaine management to us.

I knew it wasn't right, but I reasoned that we weren't really putting them in harm's way. It would just be a temporary arrangement. I was even stupid enough to believe it would help the kids with their math.

When we arrived in Orlando, Russell was more excited than the children. The travel agent had given us an itinerary for the trip so we'd be sure to see the Magic Kingdom, Epcot, Sea World and the water park. We enjoyed dinner at a difference restaurant every night, making us the family Russell had been wanting.

Despite sometimes showing signs of potential, my efforts to make Russell "good" so often failed. It was just like him to make you think he had good intentions and that he was merely flawed, and then he'd go and do something utterly indefensible. Pretty much like how when in Disney of all places he decided to teach the children how to steal. One afternoon when we decided to hang out at our hotel pool he carefully detailed to Toya, Kelisha and Rusty the art of stealing, and off to the hotel gift shop they went. Within a half hour they were back with all kinds of stolen souvenirs. Russell kept teasing them that the police were at the door looking to lock them up for shoplifting, so the children hid in the bathroom while we snorted coke. Once they came out, his reward for their success was letting them drive the rental car around the parking lot. The next day at the Magic Kingdom they continued stealing from gift shops until I started getting scared they'd get caught and told them to stop.

We did manage to break a promise to the children. We told them we'd take them to the beach when we'd driven to Miami to visit Russell's cousins, but it never happened; we were too busy getting high while the children watched television. We would've missed our flight home had I not driven the three-and-a-half hours from Miami to Orlando, feeding myself cocaine along the way so we could make it in time for our return flight.

During this time I never considered how dangerous it was to drive while under the influence, not to mention taking my eyes off the road to take a hit. I always felt that as long as my children were with me they were safe. It was ridiculous to think that, and I know now how tremendously my carelessness affected them. During this period, I just fooled myself into thinking I could control it all.

chapter nine

Gypsy
1986

My parent's neighbors had given me the nickname of
Gypsy when they saw me on the back porch, in a cloth diaper
with my face stuck to a watermelon, trying to eat through to
the rind. They saw something in me that told them my feet
wouldn't stay planted long. And they couldn't have been more
right about anything. After two years living in our apartment
on Erdrick Street, the longest we'd ever lived anywhere, the
landlord decided to sell the building. I didn't want to leave
Holmesburg; having my parents living two blocks away gave
me—and especially Kelisha—some form of stability. As usual
Russell and I waited until the last minute, having no other
choice but to move in with my oldest brother, Joe, who lived
alone in my grandmother's house one block down on the same
street.

Nanny, my maternal grandmother, had a single four-
bedroom house with a yard, which belonged to my mother and
her four sisters. The house held a lot of memories for me. I
had gone there for big family dinners, and I recall staying
there when we received the news in 1968 that Martin Luther
King had been killed. Even though Nanny died in 1972, most
of her furniture, china and antiques were still where she'd left
them, including the cup on the stove that held her used tea

bags. These things I should've cherished and respected, but my drug use clouded my judgment.

La-La agreed to let us move in, under the condition that we didn't sell drugs, as she suspected we were. I promised her we wouldn't, and Russell promised me that he would do his business in the street. I knew we were both lying—to ourselves and to La-La.

We fixed the house up with new carpet, fresh paint, curtains and replaced Nanny's furniture with our own. Gregory helped Russell install new closets, put up walls and we even made plans to replace the existing hardwood floors. We decorated Kelisha's room but decided we'd fix up the back room for Rusty when he returned from Ohio where he'd been living since our return from Disney. His return came sooner than we expected.

One evening, I received word from Gloria, Rusty's grandmother, that Sandy wanted to talk to me. With Russell sitting beside me I made the phone call.

"Brenda, I need a favor."

"What's going on?" I asked, wondering what she could possibly need from me.

"I know how much you love Rusty, and well, I need your help."

"Help with what? Is he alright?" I asked, anxious to be certain he was okay.

"Do you think you could take care of him for a little while?"

I hoped she wasn't toying with my feelings. "Me? Are you serious?"

"Well, I need you to come get him because I'm not working and me and my boyfriend are having some problems so I need some help until I get myself together."

"Are you sure?"

"What she want?" asked Russell, pestering me in the other ear.

I flagged him away and turned my attention back to Sandy.

"Are you bringing him back?"

"I want you to come get him."

"Me? Don't you think it would be better if Russell came?"

"No, my boyfriend isn't gonna go for that."

"Well, what about Eve?"

"Brenda, I want you to come. You're the one that's gonna be taking care of him."

By now my palms were sweating, and Russell was pulling on the phone trying to listen.

"Ok, if that's what you want. When do you want me to come?"

"As soon as you can."

"Alright, I'll be there tomorrow. Let me make some arrangements and I'll call you back."

"Thanks Brenda."

"No, thank you, for letting me take care of your son."

"He's your son too," Sandy said.

I never stopped to think about what her phone call meant. This woman was relinquishing her son into my care and I had taken it lightly and selfishly. I scheduled a flight for the next day, took off from work and flew to Columbus, Ohio. In my panties I stashed a plastic sandwich bag filled with a quarter ounce of coke and some joints. I wanted to be sure she didn't change her mind even if I had to pay her off. I never stopped to think about the consequences if I'd gotten caught with drugs. By this time I was a pro at transporting small quantities through the airport.

I took a cab from Columbus International to the apartment Sandy shared with her boyfriend, who ignored me when I arrived. There was no food, and the kids were sleeping on a pallet made of blankets on the living room floor. I was elated to see Rusty, but at three-years-old was a picture of sadness and neglect. He looked like a lost little boy, with clothes that were too small and didn't match, on a body that was way too frail. I prayed that Sandy had not changed her mind.

We left her apartment and walked down the street to her sister's apartment, stopping at the 7-Eleven to buy wine, beer, and sodas and hot dogs for the kids. We sat at her sister's getting high until it was time for me to catch my return flight. Through it all Sandy kept explaining to me that she was not giving her son away that she just needed some help.

My flight back home was filled with mixed emotions. I was grateful to be bringing Rusty home with me but sad for Sandy, who had to give up her son. Unable to imagine what might be going through his little mind, I did my best to reassure him that his mother loved him but needed time to, "get herself together."

I had to ask myself if I was using Rusty to replace the child I'd aborted, the son that Russell told me I had murdered. I mean, never had I been so willing to hop a plane at a moment's notice for something. If so, and if God was giving me another change to right my wrong, then I was going to love and care for Rusty like I'd given birth to him.

With our two children back together and plans for Toya to continue coming every summer, I thought we were finally settling in. Being a family wasn't just important to Russell—it was important to me, too, because that's how I'd been raised, and I felt that if we were a family, than how wrong could things get in our life?

Now that we were supposedly doing well we drew in new friends. Alicia worked with me at IBM and she and her boyfriend James became a fixture in our lives. There was plenty of excitement offered when you hung out with us, so who wouldn't want to be included? There were trips to AC where we supplied the drugs and money. There was a shootout between Russell and a neighbor because Bear kept attacking his dog. And there was Russell who had his eyes on Alicia and the three of them trying to convince me that swapping partners could be fun. I wasn't interested.

But it grew crazier when Russell called me on a Friday at work informing me that Nanny's house had been robbed. We assumed someone had climbed in through the open window in order to break the lock on our briefcase and steal the money and cocaine we stored there. They'd also cracked open Kelisha's bank and taken all of the two-dollar bills she'd been saving. Bear had been in the backyard all along—which led us to believe that whoever had robbed us must have known our dog.

We called the police and reported that money had been stolen. When the detective arrived and surveyed the scene he told us that nobody had entered through the window. He said, it had been staged and probably by someone we knew.

My brother Joe tried to tell me that Russell did it, but that seemed too far-fetched because Russell had no reason to steal from himself. Russell's version was that he and Rusty had gone to the store and asked Joe if he'd be there. Joe said yes. An hour later, when Russell returned, Joe was gone and the house had been robbed. Joe's response was that when he'd left everything was in order. Everyone had a different story. I didn't know whose side to be on, my husband's or my brother's.

For the next week my life was turned upside down. The cops came to the house in the middle of the night, looking for Russell and trying to connect him to other houses in the neighborhood that had recently been robbed.

Three days after that Russell called me at work again and said that our entire block of Erdrick Street, from Welsh Road to Rhawn Street had been barricaded and cops were outside with a bullhorn demanding that he surrender. Alicia took me home and upon arriving I found my husband handcuffed in the backseat of a police car.

That night while I waited for Russell to be released, I went to the *Holmesburg Tavern* and got into a heated argument with my brother Jeffery, accusing him of being in on the robbery. I was so spaced out on coke that Gwennie had to literally drag me home. We were standing in the enclosed porch, where she let me go ballistic for a moment, but was then forced to slap me several times across the face to get me under control.

Finally, my mother stepped in. She'd had enough. She was tired of hearing all the rumors and complaints from her sisters about what was going on in Nanny's house and told us that we had to move. I had no idea where we'd go next. We ended up in Eve's unfinished basement.

La-La and Pop-Pop weren't having their granddaughter moving into the basement of anyone's house, even if it was her grandmother. So again she was back to weekend visits.

Thus the only one who bunked down there with us was Rusty. Of course Bear made his home in the backyard. But I was so wrapped up in my own head that I didn't stop to think about the fact that I was dragging not only my daughter through the streets of Philly, but also Rusty, the child I'd promised to take care of.

Russell and I grew closer living at Eve's, because she aggravated the both of us. Besides paying rent to her, we had to give her a share of the money when we sold drugs or when she made a sale for us. Some days we had a good time together, and some days it was hell, especially when Russell and his mother would argue.

It had always been evident to me that my husband was intimidated and afraid of his mother. She knew all the right buttons to push with him. Eve often admitted that she had been physically and emotionally abusive to her children when they were growing up. She said it was to keep them in line since their father hadn't been around. I guess there was a thin line between ass whippings and abuse. One you did because a child misbehaved and the other you did out of frustration for what was going on in your own life. I was familiar with the latter through her son.

Through all of it, Eve was still Russell's biggest fan, and all her children knew it, as did his women. He could do no wrong in her eyes. If he did do something questionable, she'd always defend him, by saying that it must not have been intentional because "he *really* does have a good heart."

As for my relationship with Eve I took whatever part of our love/hate relationship she was dealing out for the day in hopes that one day I'd be a good girl in her eyes, not the one who had stolen her cousin's man or the one who'd slept with her daughter's boyfriend.

chapter ten

Toxic
1986

I knew at some point something had to give and I would be made aware of how my ridiculous lifestyle couldn't continue in such a state. The first thing I noticed through the fog that my life had become was the deterioration of my performance at work. IBM didn't have a set amount of sick days one could take. It was unlimited—to be used with discretion, but what did I know about that? For me it was one illness after another: migraines, cramps, sick kids, a car accident, whatever excuse I could think of to get out of work for the day. I'd also failed at a communications class I'd attended in Atlanta because I was more focused on exploring the city's nightlife than my class work.

Two months of living with Eve was about all we could take. We rented a three-bedroom townhouse in International City, which was located at 84th and Lindbergh Boulevard. It was a community of middle class black families and professional athletes.

The plan had been for the children to attend school from their grandparents' houses and come home with us on the weekends, but that only lasted a month. It began to nag me when I would be leaving for work in the morning and see the suburban mothers sending their children off to school. I longed to have my children with me. I wanted to feed them breakfast, tuck Rusty's shirt into his pants and braid Kelisha's hair. After much negotiation we talked our parents into letting us have the children back. Wanting the best education for them, they were enrolled in Evelyn Graves Christian Academy at 56th and Chester Avenue in Southwest Philly. They hated it.

They hadn't been there a month when I received a call from the principal that Rusty was in class singing the beer commercial, "I'm gonna be a Moosehead man tonight," which we thought was funny. Kelisha complained that in order to use the bathroom she had to raise her hand and then walk to the front of the class to get toilet paper. Our children also refused to ride in the school's transportation, an old station wagon.

By November we pulled them out, and using Jena's address I enrolled Kelisha, who was about 9 years old, in one of the better public schools: Greenfield, at 22nd and Chestnut Streets in center city. 4-year-old Rusty was enrolled in a preschool at 57th and Vine Streets. My routine in the mornings, after having been up late most nights, would be to take a cab to Eve's, drop off Rusty, then continue downtown with Kelisha where I'd drop her off before going to work.

The holidays rolled around and, as was typical, I attended the annual IBM holiday luncheon. What I hadn't shared with my husband was that earlier in the week I'd manipulated my parents into relinquishing to me the children's savings bonds, with the false intent of re-investing them. Instead I cashed them and had Rick, my co-worker, take me to see Russell's suppliers—I purchased an ounce of coke from Skinny Jimmy and a quarter pound of weed from the Booty Man. After picking up my two packages, we went to Rick's house and spent the next few hours freebasing and drinking Hennessy.

Needing an excuse, I made another stop at Renée's house in Southwest Philly in case Russell asked where I'd been. The truth was I was scared to go home. Renée knew this and knew that Russell would probably kick my ass when I got there. What I didn't know was that once I left she'd phoned the police. When I finally made it home it was around 11:00 p.m.

and Russell was enraged.

"Brenda, where the fuck you been?" he asked from the landing of the stairs.

Trying to avoid his eyes, I focused on Kelisha and Rusty who sat behind him on the step watching us.

"I was at the luncheon, you know that," I answered casually, taking off my coat.

"I didn't have my keys. Shit, I was locked out the house for two hours," he responded as he walked down the steps, his hands behind his back.

"I'm sorry, I forgot," I said, having no recollection of the conversation.

"I wanted us to take the kids out to dinner and your ass been in the damn street!" he said, his face strained.

"You knew I had the Christmas luncheon to go to. Why you acting like that?" I asked, unsure if it was real or if the drugs were fooling me into believing that the reason Russell had his hands behind his back was to keep from hitting me.

"You ain't been at no luncheon all this time. Look at you," he said, referring to the awful habit I had of gritting my teeth when I was high on cocaine.

I removed the two packages from my purse and dropped them on the coffee table. "Russell, I stopped to get this."

"Where'd you get the money?" he asked.

"I used some of the kids' savings bonds and Rick took me."

When he bent over to inspect the coke I noticed that behind his back he was holding the 22-inch Katana sword that was usually kept above the entryway. Realizing that he was possibly considering hacking me to death I looked at the children and said, "Kelisha and Rusty yall go upstairs."

"You took somebody with you to Jimmy's and the Booty Man's?" he asked while lightly tapping the sword against his thigh.

I backed away from him and moved closer to the front door.

"No, he waited outside."

"That's bullshit. You know you were wrong, don't you?"

I didn't answer. My mouth wouldn't stop twitching, so I shook my head yes.

Russell dipped his pinky finger into the coke and took a hit up one nostril, then the other. I wanted to do the same but was afraid to ask.

"Take this and get your ass upstairs," he told me, handing me the packages. I stuffed them back into my purse and headed toward the stairs.

There was a hard knock on the front door.

"WHO IS IT?" Russell asked in his booming voice.

"THE POLICE. OPEN UP!"

"Who the fuck—" Russell began to say when I bounded down the steps, running past him to open the door.

"Mrs. Douglass?"

"Yes?" I said, praying the officer couldn't tell I was high.

"We heard there was a disturbance," he said, his eyes darting behind me to where Russell stood.

"No we're alright. It was just an argument," I told him, since Russell hadn't actually hit me.

He nodded towards Russell and asked, "And you sir?"

"I'm fine. Ain't nothing going on."

"Well if you're sure everything's alright."

"Yes, we're good," I said and closed the door, wondering if Russell would now hit me because the police had showed up.

Kelisha and Rusty had returned to the stairs so I led them back to their room. After tucking them in bed I told Kelisha that if her father began hitting me, she was to call the cops. I never stopped to think that she was a child whom I was now making responsible for my safety. Wasn't it supposed to be the other way around?

Once Russell and I were in bed he wasn't in the mood to get high, nor did he respond to my attempts at having sex. During some failed foreplay, the doorbell rang. This time it was my brother Gregory.

"What the hell is going on Russell?" my brother asked, as the three of us stood in the living room.

"Nothing man, we alright," Russell said.

He looked me over for any signs that I'd been hit.

"Kizzy called Daddy and said you two were fighting."

"No we weren't. We just had an argument. It was my fault. I didn't get home till late."

"You need to get out of here for the night until Russell cools off."

"I ain't touched your sister Greg."

"Let's go Brenda."

"Okay," I said, pulling my coat over top of my nightgown as Kelisha did the same, while Rusty attempted to follow.

"I hope you don't think you're taking my son with you."

"Why not?"

"He ain't yours, remember?"

Of course I remembered because on every occasion he reminded me. And if he didn't keep that fresh in my head then Eve certainly did.

Rusty sat back down on the steps in his underwear.

I stayed with my parents for the next week, trying to convince myself not to return. I'd taken the coke and weed with me which meant I didn't have to share any of the profits with my husband. However, with pressure from him that I'd deserted him and Rusty, I apologized for leaving and went home to take what I knew would be my punishment.

It was right before Christmas when I'd had enough of Russell's beatings. One Thursday morning, after dropping the children off at school, I went in to talk with my manager, Laney. There were no visible bruises, but on this day I was distraught from a night of getting high and fighting. I was nowhere near ready to tell the truth about what really went on in my life, so I told her that I was afraid to go home because Russell had threatened me with violence. She offered her assistance by putting me up at the Holiday Inn at 18th and Market Streets to allow me time to get myself together. I was able to quickly put a plan into action—one of my co-workers had a sister who worked at the Wanamaker House at 21st and Walnut Streets. I looked at the 18th floor studio and signed the lease, having no intention of telling Russell my plans.

My warped sense of thinking had me believing that this was my chance to start fresh with my daughter, whom Russell couldn't take away from me as he often threatened to do with Rusty. I always thought the solution to my problems was to run away from them, but what I didn't realize was that I was running in a circle that always led right back to Russell.

The first night at the hotel defeated its purpose, because rather than figure out how I was going to "get myself together," I spent the evening getting high with my co-workers while Kelisha sat on the opposite bed pretending to watch television.

It was the following morning while I was at work that Russell went to Kelisha's school and removed her from class so she could show him where we were staying. He continued to call me, and I ignored him until after I'd taken Kelisha to my parents' house which is when Russell showed up at my hotel room door. I felt like I had the upper hand because he was never abusive when he wanted me back so over a room service dinner I expressed to him that I would no longer put up with his abuse. But what did it all mean if we were chasing shots of Hennessy with lines of cocaine? By Saturday morning I'd agreed to let him move in with us.

It was the beginning of January when we began moving from our townhouse in International City to the Wannamaker House in center city. Hoping my parents would understand why I was moving again, I told them my plans when I went to visit.

"Uhm, me and Russell got a new place."

"What do you mean?" my father asked.

"Well we want to move closer to the city."

"Bones I don't understand why you keep staying with that nigga. I told you a long time ago he wasn't no damn good."

"Dad, he's not like that anymore." I lied.

"All this moving around—what are you trying to do to Kizzy?"

"Nothing. She'll be closer to school. Greenfield is right down the street."

"I'm not gonna let you keep dragging my granddaughter around the city."

"You hurt me to my heart when you went back to that boy

after what he did to you in North Carolina," my mother stated, adding further emphasis by holding her hand to her heart. Brenda are you crazy?" she asked.

"What are you talking about?"

"She's right, Bones. What is this, the 8th, 9th, 10th, time you've moved since she was a baby? You're going to mess that child's life up."

"No I won't. She'll be alright."

My mother stood up, one hand on her hip, the other with her finger in my face.

"I'm telling you right now damn it; if you don't let us keep Kizzy here I'm taking you to court."

"What do you mean?" I asked, while actually looking at my father for reassurance that she wasn't serious.

"You heard me. I'm not gonna let you ruin her life. You either leave her here or I'm going downtown and taking you to court for custody."

I didn't know what to say, because it was clear that my parents didn't trust me to properly care for their granddaughter. And as much as I hated to admit it, they were right. Hell, they'd always been right; it was me who'd been wrong. They'd really been the ones raising her anyway. Whose child stays at their parents during the week and only comes on the weekend? It wasn't the better school system, because if that were the case we should have been living in the right district. They were taking her from me because I'd proved unable to provide a safe and secure living situation for her.

"Dad?"

"That's right, Bones. You leave her here with us. Your mother ain't sleeping at night as it is worrying about Kizzy."

I relented, knowing I'd lost my daughter.

Not only did Kelisha go to stay with La-La and Pop-Pop, but Rusty went to live with Eve. The guilt of losing my children could only mean an impeding disaster; because what our parents didn't realize was that they shouldn't have trusted us on the weekends either.

chapter eleven

The Wannamaker House
January, 1987

Russell and I now lived in center city. We were two blocks from Rittenhouse Square, and our 18th-floor windows overlooked the Schuylkill River. The building provided us with amenities like a rooftop pool, exercise facilities, sauna, Jacuzzi, parking garage, and a doorman. Our new residence, combined with our drug use, had reached a point of making us believe we had succeeded at something when in reality our lives were only a few months from exploding.

Russell and I were no longer individuals; we were now one. The only time we weren't together was when we went to work, and we wouldn't be doing that much longer. We spent so much time together that we'd begun to look alike. With the exception, of course, that he'd grown a beard. To me, it made him look even fiercer when he was enraged.

In a continuing effort to help me, my manager, Laney, offered me the opportunity to work a special assignment for IBM's litigation office while they were embroiled in a lawsuit. The office at 5th and Chestnut Streets was staffed around-the-clock by lawyers and staffers from Philadelphia and New York. My role was that of legal typist, and my hours were from 7:00 p.m. to 7:00 a.m., which included catered breakfasts, lunches and dinners. Limousines and cab vouchers were also available for business-related transportation.

I had never worked at night, and the only way I knew to adjust to staying awake was to snort cocaine throughout my time in the office. This also meant that in the morning when I got off I couldn't sleep, so I'd pop two Xanax. I didn't think this was a problem, because I knew what to take and when to take it, and I figured that once I grew accustomed to my new hours, my body would adjust and I could cut back on the drugs. I told myself that until this point, I had only used drugs recreationally, and the consistent use of them for work was more like medication than getting high.

It wasn't long before two of my coworkers, Brian and Sheila, noticed what I was into and that we had something in common. I was the fool to think that nobody else noticed my extended lunches, sniffling nose, frequent trips to the ladies' room and constant nervous chatter.

One night Sheila was getting off work as I was taking a dinner break, we decided to stop across the street at a bar in the Bourse building for happy hour. After several drinks and a few trips to the ladies' room, Sheila began to talk about the sexual trysts in which she and her husband had participated. That gave me an idea. For months Russell had been bugging me to have a threesome, but I kept turning him down. Now here was Sheila, attractive, mature; so I asked her if she would be interested in a ménage a trois. She said she was all for it, depending on what Russell looked like. I knew she wouldn't be disappointed.

With this opportunity in front of me, there was no way I was going back to work. I called the litigation office and told my supervisor that Sheila was suffering from food poisoning and I was taking her home. Then I called Russell and told him I had someone for him to meet.

When he arrived at the bar I introduced Russell to Sheila and then took him into the bathroom to fill him in on my idea. He was excited about the idea but he couldn't believe I was finally agreeing. What Russell didn't know was that this wouldn't be the first time I'd been with a woman; it would, however, be the first time I'd shared one with my husband.

We left the bar together, but Russell of course had to make some stops before going home so we could make everything right. We went off in Sheila's Corvette to the Booty Man's and Skinny Jimmy's for two packages. By the time we arrived in front of the Wanamaker House, an intoxicated Sheila had changed her mind. Not wanting to disappoint Russell, I encouraged her to at least come in and get high for a while. She was unable to turn down that offer.

Inside the apartment Russell got a mirror and used a razor to set up long lines of coke for us. I rolled up a few joints and the party commenced.

"Why don't yall get undressed," Russell suggested, after we became relaxed.

"Okay, where's the bathroom?" Sheila asked.

When she returned Russell was sitting on the bed in his underwear, and I was sitting naked on the couch.

"What you wanna do?" Russell asked me, anxious to get started.

"I wanna get high first," I said, as if I already wasn't high enough.

Sheila took a toke off the joint Russell passed her, then sat on the floor between my legs. With Russell watching she reached up with her hands and massaged my breasts.

"Brenda, come here for a minute," Russell said, motioning for me to follow him into the kitchen.

"What's up?" I asked, thinking he'd changed his mind.

"Look, I don't care what you do but don't kiss her in the mouth or eat her pussy."

"Don't worry, I'm not," I said, realizing Russell wanted the attention.

When we were back in the living room I had a plan to put him more at ease.

"Russell why don't you lay on the bed?"

"Alright. What y'all gonna do?" he asked.

"Yeah, lay down," Sheila told him.

Not sure if I could handle her making love to my husband, I decided the best way was to be bold. "Why don't you suck his dick?"

"Brenda, you sure?" Russell asked, surprised at my suggestion, yet wasting no time arranging himself spread-eagle across the bed.

"Yeah, go head. I don't care."

With her eyes on Russell, Sheila grabbed the base of his dick, knelt between his legs and took him in her mouth.

I could see from where I was sitting that Sheila had given him a solid erection. Russell then nodded his head for me to come to them. I sat beside him on the bed where he leaned over and began licking my nipples.

"Get up on it," he told Sheila.

A woman I barely knew was riding my husband with a steady stride when all of sudden Russell went soft inside her.

"What happened?" she asked, looking from me to him.

"Hold up," Russell said, pushing her off and looking puzzled that he was having a problem staying hard.

"What's wrong?" I asked, feeling bothered that they were interrupting my lacing another joint with coke.

"Nothing. Pass me that glass," Russell said, pointing to the glass of Courvoisier he had been drinking.

Russell swallowed a big gulp and got up to sit on the couch. Having been presented with the opportunity for a threesome, he was desperate to perform, but it was useless—Sheila was now uninterested. Frustrated, she proceeded to get dressed.

"Look, I'm going to leave," she said. "This isn't working out."

Wanting to keep Russell occupied so I could continue snorting coke, I said, "Don't leave yet. Let's try something else."

"Yeah, check it out, take your clothes off and let me fuck you from the back," Russell told Sheila, hoping to regain his hard on.

"Is it alright with you, Brenda?" she asked.

"I don't care—whatever he wants," I replied, satisfied that Russell wasn't putting a limit on the amount of coke I was snorting.

Sheila removed her clothes. This time she bent over the

side of the bed, her ass in the air. Now on his knees, Russell was able to put his semi-hard dick inside her, but when he attempted to pump it went limp. I almost wanted to laugh, but that would've been a death sentence.

"Awww shit, it must be from the coke," Russell said, looking down at a dick that wasn't cooperating.

Sheila turned her attentions toward me and said, "Whatever, but I still wanna fuck her."

I laughed it off and went to roll a joint because I knew Russell wasn't going for that.

Russell stepped into his jeans and said, "Forget it."

While Russell walked Sheila to the lobby, I sat on the couch getting high, confident I'd have no problem satisfying my husband.

"I can't believe you wanted me to fuck that ole' bitch," he commented when he walked back into the apartment.

I lit a joint, puffed and passed it to him. "I thought that's what you wanted. Anyway she's not that old. You said she looked good."

"Yeah, but that's probably why my dick wouldn't get hard, cause she was too old."

"It's damn sure the first time I ever seen your dick not get hard."

"How about you suck my dick like you know how?" he said, gesturing with his dick for me to come to him.

I took two big snorts of coke then proceeded to give my husband back his manhood.

The next morning Russell had an appointment with his physical therapist because of his Workmen's Compensation case. I was glad he didn't ask me to go with him because my body was aching from being up all night and all I wanted to do was sleep. However, when he returned two hours later I wished I had gone.

Before he came in the darkened living room he yelled out to me.

"Who's been over here?"

"What? Nobody. I been sleep."

"Who the fuck's hair is this on the towel?" he asked,

walking into the living room.

"Shit, I don't know. It's probably from those washing machines," I said, peeking out from under the covers, still unconcerned.

"Yeah right! It looks like Sheila's to me. You sure she didn't come over here while I was gone?"

"Are you crazy?" I asked, pissed that his paranoia was kicking in while I was hung over.

"No, now you git the fuck up."

I rolled over and sat naked on the side of the bed. He was towering over me, giving me no room to get away from him.

"Now tell me the truth. Was she over here while I was at therapy?"

"No Russell," I responded, wondering where the hell he came up with this stuff.

"Didn't she say last night that she was gonna fuck you? And don't think I didn't notice that that bitch was a dyke, that's probably why my dick wouldn't get hard."

"Russell I don't want her, and I damn sure wouldn't have nobody over here."

Without warning he hit me with a backhand across the face. It sent me reeling into the wall.

I was fully awake now.

"RUSSELL, WHAT'S WRONG WITH YOU? I did that last night because you wanted to, and I'd never cheat on you. Com'on now stop!"

"You gone tell me the fuckin' truth. Now get the fuck over here."

I didn't want to leave whatever false security the wall provided, but I knew that it would be worse if he had to come get me. I scooted back to the edge of the bed, but before I could stand up he wrapped his right hand around my neck, lifting me into the air.

"Brenda, you better tell me the fucking truth," he said, his face as hard as the chokehold he had on me.

"You want a fuckin' woman don't you?" he asked me through clenched teeth.

He was asking me questions, but how could I answer when

I couldn't even breathe? I shook my head no and felt his grasp loosen.

"No Russell, I want you. Com'on, let me suck your dick, please."

He dropped me back down onto the bed.

"Oh, now you wanna suck my dick. Well, how did it taste last night after I had my dick in her?"

"Russell, stop it—please don't say that," I said, lowering my head in disgust at his question. But who had time to dwell on that? I had to save myself.

He removed his pants and boxers. "Well, suck my dick then."

There was no way I could return to work with Russell having accused me of sleeping with Sheila. It also would have been an embarrassment to return so soon to my regular job at IBM, so I came up with a plan. I called my supervisor at the litigation office and told him I'd fallen and sprained my ankle while running for a taxi in the snow. I further cemented my story by visiting one of Russell's doctors and getting a note for some time off. That's when I received a call directly from Laney who told me that when I was released from the doctor's care that I was to return to the office at 17th and Market Streets.

This would be the first time I'd ever been out of work with Russell. By now my life was moving so fast I couldn't keep up. The amount of drugs I was ingesting and my lack of sleep were tearing my body apart. There were Friday nights that I was too high to pick up the kids. My mother would call, and I'd make excuses about why I was running late, insisting that I was on my way. When I'd show up the following day my mother would be sure to tell me how Kelisha would stay awake waiting for me, watching every car headlight that turned the bend to see if it was me. What my parents did notice was that I'd begun to lose weight and that my eyes were always red and hollow.

The weekend visits from the children didn't even cause a pause in our lifestyle. If we had company we'd put the children in the tub for a bubble bath until we finished getting high. One time we even made them eat pizza while taking a bath. If I wasn't home Russell would either leave the kids by themselves while he made a run, or take them with him.

On one occasion, Russell took the kids with him to the Badlands at 8th and Butler Streets to pick up a package. While making his purchase, a gun battle broke out with bullets flying over the car. This scared Russell, and me too when he told me the story. It also was an alert that something was wrong—that we'd put our children in jeopardy. Russell felt he'd been totally irresponsible putting his children in danger and determined that we had a problem.

Russell decided that maybe we were getting high too much. He also had me call IBM's benefits department asking to have them mail me information on their Employee Assistance Program. When the information came he read it and called the hotline explaining that we were having a problem with getting high too much. They made an appointment for us to see a psychologist the following week, but when the day came we never bothered to show up, this time or the next two times.

It was late February when we woke up to Russell's sister Jena's screaming voice. Somehow she'd gotten into the apartment and we hadn't even heard her. The apartment was strewn with clothes, money and drugs. I had a busted lip and a black eye, and Russell had scratches all over his face.

"WHAT THE FUCK IS WRONG WITH Y'ALL? LOOK AT THIS PLACE! Y'ALL ARE OUT OF CONTROL!"

We couldn't answer. We just laid there, staring up at her, not knowing how long we'd been there.

"I'M OUTTA HERE. Y'ALL ARE DISGUSTING. YOU NEED TO GET SOME FUCKIN' HELP!"

chapter twelve

Detox
March, 1987

Keeping the next appointment Russell made with the EAP office, we met a young Jewish psychologist at her office in the Dorchester on Rittenhouse Square.

"What brought you here today?" she asked, after we'd been seated in her office.

"What do you mean?" I asked arrogantly, not wanting to be there.

"Well, you called me several times. I'm assuming there is a problem of some sort," she said, looking from me to my husband.

Russell spoke up. "It's not a problem. I don't know, maybe, but we just been getting high too much and we need to find a way to slow down."

"What do you get high on?"

"We smoke joints, snort coke, drink, the usual," I answered, thinking it might make her back off.

"How often?"

I wanted to say as often as we could, but instead I answered with, "Everyday, I guess."

"How long has this been going on?"

"I don't know maybe about 10, 15 years, but not this much."

"Mr. Douglass, from what I could tell from your phone call

and from what you and your wife have told me today, it certainly has all the signs of an addiction."

"No, it's not like that. We just like to party too much and it's gotten out of control."

"Do you have any children?"

"Yes, but they're fine, they live with our parents," I offered, having no idea how ridiculous I sounded.

"And I assume you work?"

"That's how we got here," I said.

"Your job sent you?"

"No, we came on our own."

"But you're both not working at the moment."

"We're out because of injuries," Russell told her.

"I see."

"What's that?" Russell asked.

"I'm listening to everything you're saying, and I'm of the opinion that you both need to seek in-patient treatment at a rehabilitation facility."

I couldn't believe what I was hearing; this woman actually thought we were junkies. How could that be so? We still looked good, hadn't sold our material things and even though the children weren't with us, they were being taken good care of. My reasoning was she was saying that because we were Black.

"Look, lady—you have us mixed up with the wrong people. We're not junkies. Look at us. I have two children and a good job."

"And what if you lose it all?" she asked.

I turned my head away from her, struck with the reality that I'd already lost my children.

"All I'm suggesting is that you visit with an in-patient facility, have a conversation with the director and see what you think."

"I'm not doing it Russell! I mean, what will people say? All we need to do is slow down, you'll see."

I never bothered to mention that I might've noticed a problem when I found myself in the laundry room one night, scraping the remains of coke out of the red grinder we used to crush the rocks to a smooth powder.

"Brenda maybe we should look into it."

"I'm sorry I wasn't able to help, but if you change your mind please give me a call."

It only took another week before we made a desperate late-night call to her office. She referred us to Charter Fairmount Institute for an interview.

The morning of that appointment we dressed in our finest we-don't-look-like-junkies attire. Our arms and necks were adorned with gold, with Russell in his black leather trench and me with my fur and a fresh jheri curl.

At no time during the interview at Fairmount did the director point his finger at us and tell us that we were junkies. He skillfully allowed us to dig our own hole until we almost got into an argument. There were a few factors that came out during that interview: the length of time we'd been getting high; the amount of drugs we used on a daily basis; both of our jobs being at risk and the obvious fact that we didn't trust to be out of each others sight.

It was evident to him—and somewhat to us—that we'd never be able to slow down in our present environment. We still defended ourselves, however, and tried to make him see that maybe being outpatients would work for us, but I knew we'd been exposed.

"Listen, why don't I let the two of you talk alone and then you tell me your decision? I'll be in the hallway."

"What do you think Russell?"

"I don't know. I mean it doesn't sound that bad, at least we'll be together."

"Yeah, but what are people going to say? I don't want nobody to know I'm in a rehab. That shit ain't right," I told him, referring to the people we got high with as if they even mattered.

"We don't have to tell nobody. They can think we're on vacation."

"Well I don't want to have to stop *everything*."

"Me neither."

"So how we gonna do that?"

"I'll tell you right now Brenda, I might give up the coke and stuff but you know I still like to drink."

"Then if you're gonna still do that, I'm definitely not going to stop smoking weed."

"Why don't we just come in here to chill out for a little while? We might even be able to save some money."

"You're right. It'll be like a vacation."

Keeping our pride intact, we told everyone except our parents that IBM was sending me to Florida for a month and Russell was going with me. Kelisha was disappointed, because I'd promised her that the next time I went away she could go with me. Since I was still out for my fake injury, I didn't bother to mention it to Laney. I just had the doctor write me an extended medical absence note.

The day we were to check into Fairmount, we decided to spend it getting high on anything and everything we could get our hands on. Russell's brother Juan came over in the morning and cooked us breakfast. I didn't think it was gourmet to have home fries, eggs and bacon doused with wine but what the hell? We then rode all over the city picking up coke, weed and stopping in bars to drink.

It was about 7:00 p.m. when we finally made our way out Ridge Avenue to Fairmount Institute, stopping for our last drink of Remy Martin with a Moosehead chaser at Anthony's Tavern, a few blocks from the facility. I remember Russell saying to me, "Brenda, I know you'll never tell me the truth, but I know the only reason you fucked Tony was because I took his sister to Charlotte."

It was six years later and he was still hanging onto that. However, I wasn't stupid enough to believe that he wouldn't kick my butt if I told him the truth.

When we turned into the parking lot at Fairmount, we found a closed administration building, so we went to the first building that had lights on. The nurse at the front desk stopped us in the foyer.

"Can I help you?" she asked.

"Yes, we're the Douglass'," I answered in my professional IBM voice like I was showing up for a business conference.

She looked us over, as did the other residents who were beginning to mill around us.

"We were expecting you this morning," she said.

"Well, they said 9:00 and we didn't know if it meant morning or night and now we're here," Russell responded.

"I don't know if we can accept you tonight. You're going to have to wait until the morning. Plus, it looks like you've been drinking."

At this Russell became aggravated.

"Yeah, we been getting high! This is rehab ain't it? That's why we're here—to stop getting high."

The nurse began telling the other patients to move on.

"I'll have to give you a Breathalyzer test."

"Whatever," Russell replied.

She tested me first, then Russell.

"You are way above the toxic level. The best I can do is send you to detox, probably at Chestnut Hill Hospital.

"I ain't going no damn where. Com'on Brenda, let's go home," Russell insisted.

"Wait a minute, Russell. We're here now, let's go with it and see what happens."

Upon reaching Chestnut Hill we signed ourselves in at the registration desk. An orderly escorted us upstairs to a locked unit of the hospital. Next stop was the nurse's station where we had to complete additional paperwork.

There were a few people on the detox unit with us, mostly women who were wandering by, using the phone, looking at us, and saying hello. I barely responded. Russell had already been to the community room, met a few people and checked the place over, clearly he was ready for this detox and recovery thing; I was not. To me the people appeared tired and bland and the unit smelled like cough syrup and alcohol. I told myself that I didn't have it as bad as them, because I still looked good and, for the most part, felt good.

We were then shown to separate sleeping rooms, located at opposite ends of the hall. I complained about it to the nurse, telling her that they'd told us at Fairmount that we'd be in the same room. Her response was that this wasn't rehab, it was

115

detox, and not only would we be in separate rooms, but we weren't allowed in each other's room. I let it go, since Russell reminded me that we'd only be there overnight. After we unpacked, they allowed us time to talk. It was then that I passed Russell one of two Xanax I'd found in my pocket.

After undressing and showering in the tiny bathroom, I pulled the children's pictures out of my suitcase and placed them on the nightstand next to the Bible. I remembered the day Kelisha was born and how I'd promised that I'd take good care of her. I'd tried, but the drugs got in the way—or in truth, she'd gotten in the way of the drugs, and I'd pushed her aside, allowing me to end up in this place.

I tried to look out the window before getting in bed but I couldn't see well through the rusted mesh wire that locked it shut. I got down on my knees, said my prayers and climbed into the narrow hospital bed. I lay there thinking about where I was and asking myself what the hell I was doing there. Detox was for drunks and junkies, not me. I wasn't living on the street in dirty, funky clothes; I had a good job, beautiful children and a husband. Maybe I got high too much, but I didn't need to be in detox.

I looked over at Rusty and Kelisha's pictures and wondered what they would think of their mother if they knew where I really was and why. I thought of how terrible they would think I was, and then I began to wonder how awful I really must be. I asked myself how I could take care of Rusty any better than Sandy, since I'd ended up in detox.

The nurse came by on her rounds, saw I was tossing and turning and asked me if I was okay. I told her I wasn't, that I wanted to see my husband. A few minutes later Russell appeared in the doorway.

"What's wrong?" he whispered smiling at me.

"I wanna leave. I don't wanna be here," I said, holding back tears from where I sat on the side of the bed.

"You'll be alright."

"I can't sleep. How long do we have to stay here?"

"Three to five days, they said."

"Bullshit, nobody said anything about that. What about the

kids? I wanna talk to them."

"You can call them in the morning, Brenda."

I began crying and he opened his arms to me. I let him hold me, hoping he could make all of this go away.

"I gotta go back to my room. They said I could only stay five minutes."

"I hate this place and I'm not staying here no five fuckin' days!"

"You'll be alright. I love you," he said, then kissed me on the cheek.

"I love you, too."

At 3:00 a.m. I was still unable to sleep. All I could think about was the mess I'd made of my life.

I called for the nurse, who said she'd get something for me. How I wished it would be a joint or a warm glass of cognac. She returned with four large white pills and told me they would help. I asked her what they were and she told me they were L-Tryptophan. I took the large pills thinking they wouldn't work for me, but I finally fell asleep.

The next morning I showered and dressed, determined to look good. I didn't want these people to think I had a problem. Russell kept sticking his head in my door and I was getting annoyed at him for laughing this thing off, but at this point he was all I had. The nurse announced that breakfast would be served shortly and that we should come to the dining room. I moisturized and activated my hair, put on makeup and my Poison perfume, and dressed in jeans, a sweatshirt and matching headband.

Russell waited for me outside my door, and we walked to the makeshift dining room for our first breakfast in detox. We sat at the table as the others walked in and sat down. I thought all the women looked like shit. Most of them were White, but there was one Black girl next to me. I knew I had to be better off than they were.

After we were all seated, they rolled in an old man in a wheelchair. The food was then brought in on trays that had nameplates, and we began eating. I tried to eat, but it was awful. The eggs and bacon had no taste, and even salt and pepper didn't

117

help. I settled for the toast and coffee. The other people introduced themselves and tried to be friendly. Then the old man started gagging and one of the girls wheeled him into the bathroom, which was inside the dining room, where he commenced to throw up. They said not to let it bother us, because he threw up at every meal. We were given the menu and told that we could order what we liked for lunch and dinner—not that there was much to choose from—but by that point I'd lost my appetite.

After breakfast I returned to my room, not wanting to be bothered with anyone, and especially not wanting to go into the community room. Russell came by and asked me if I was ready to call the kids. That was about the only thing I was ready for. I talked to La-La and Pop-Pop and told them why we were at detox instead of rehab and then I talked to Kelisha, whom I was still lying to that we were in Florida. By the time I finished I was choked up and had to pull myself together before we called Eve's. Russell called and told Eve our whereabouts, and I talked with Rusty, who wanted to know when we were coming home. After our conversation I went back to my room, lay across the bed and felt sorry for myself.

Since it was the weekend, we didn't have much of a structured day. The nurse came by and told me that I might feel better if I went into the community room and talked with the other patients. Russell didn't appear to have a problem adjusting, but I only felt comfortable in a chair in a far corner of the room. I listened to one woman who was a nurse talk about how she would go into work drugged up, and write her own prescriptions. When the hospital finally caught up with her she was forced into rehab to save her job. However, she still didn't believe she had a problem. Hell, even I could see that she did.

Then there was the spoiled rich Italian girl, who was a nervous wreck. She'd been on pills, coke, crank and alcohol. Her pills were all doctor-prescribed; most days she took at least 12 varieties. Here in detox she was on heavy doses of Valium to keep her nerves from cracking up.

The Black girl was addicted to smoking crack and talked

about how she had neglected her children and would have done anything to get high. How could she neglect her children? Surely I'd told myself I hadn't been that bad.

The movies we watched had a greater effect on me than the personal stories, because I began to realize how drugs and alcohol could really destroy a person's health and that drinking alcohol was no different from taking drugs. Watching them really made me crave getting high. I laughed the movies off on the outside but called myself a fool when I thought about all the shit I'd ingested.

The only thing Russell didn't handle well was when the group discussed domestic violence. His stern look dared me to mention that I'd ever been abused.

There were no outside privileges until one day the administrator decided that we'd been on good behavior and agreed to let us go for a walk around the grounds. It was good to be in fresh air, because it was March and the air was cool and crisp. I had begun to get suspicious that Russell was having sex with the Italian girl, especially since his room was directly across from hers and I'd seen him coming out of there. When I mentioned it he told me that I was paranoid.

I built a bond with the women during those five days. I even began helping the old man. As we departed to go to our individual rehabs, we vowed to keep in touch. Even though I realized I had some things in common with these people, I still felt I had it more together than they did.

The harsher reality was that I was 29-years-old, and about to enter a drug rehab facility. The only thing that made me stay on course for the next 30 days was the thought that I could finally get to a good place with Russell and my children, if we were both clean.

chapter thirteen

Fairmount Institute
1987

Fairmount was a beautifully landscaped facility neatly tucked away off Ridge Avenue in Roxborough. There were four housing units: adults, young adults, adolescents and one for mental patients. The remainder of the buildings included an administration and medical building, a dining/meeting hall and a lecture hall where there was a gym located in the basement. The only thing missing was a swimming pool. All these buildings were spread out among the grounds and accessible by foot.

It was Spring and the smell of the fresh cut grass and flowers was breathtaking. There were basketball and tennis courts, a football field, a garden and a greenhouse. One of the homes nearby even had horses that were usually out to pasture. We were shown to our room, which made people whisper, since Russell and I were allowed to share a room. This had been unheard of in the past. Ours was one of the first buildings built, and it was more like a big house divided into numerous bedrooms and offices. There were two television rooms, a nurse's station, a small library and a few offices on each floor. There were four floors and Russell and I were on the basement floor in a corner room that smelled like Pine Sol. We both had a hard time accepting the fact that nobody was getting high.

After we unpacked a female psych tech came to our room and went through our things, removing what we couldn't have. For instance, she took my perfume (thinking I'd drink it for alcohol), Russell's razor, in case he was suicidal or homicidal, the 13" television/radio we'd brought and numerous other things that we would've used for nothing other than their actual purpose. As she looked through our things, she asked us if we thought we were going on a vacation.

Our daily agenda included two lectures, group therapy with a counselor, individual therapy with a psychiatrist, an NA or AA meeting every night, occupational activities, three meals a day and television until 11:00 p.m. At that time it was lights out, and yes, they expected Russell and I to sleep in separate beds.

Once we settled in, we had to meet with our individual treatment teams. Russell met with his first, and then it was my turn. With the exception of Dylan, the counselors weren't too tough on me. Dylan wanted to know why I always referred to Kelisha as *my* daughter rather than *our* daughter. My response was that I didn't know why. I'd never thought about it, but maybe it was because Russell had three children and I wanted to distinguish Kelisha as belonging to me.

We thought the first few days were fun, listening to people talk about themselves and what they'd done. The lectures were interesting and I even noticed some similarities between my life and the things others revealed. I figured I'd take the info and use it when I needed it. But it didn't turn out to be that simple.

After about two weeks things began to change. While sitting in the corner of a women's meeting listening to the other women "share" I suddenly realized that if I wanted to stay free from drugs, I would have to do more than give up coke and alcohol, I would also have to stop smoking joints. That scared me. I felt confused and began to withdraw from the group, looking at the others as if they were trying to pull me into a cult. I admitted I'd carried the coke thing a little too far, but there couldn't be anything wrong with smoking weed. Hell, that helped me; it helped me calm down when I was too hyped and to forget when I didn't want to deal with reality. And now they were saying I had to give that up. It was a rude awakening. I didn't say anything to anyone, but after group was over I went to the phone booth and called my friend Renée. In between tears I told her where I was and what was going on. She kept telling me that everything would be alright. Russell walked up as I was hanging up the phone.

"Who you talking to? You're not supposed to be on the phone."

I started to lie and say it was my father, but I was too afraid he'd see the lie across my face. I told him the truth.

"Renée."

"What you call her for?"

I shrugged my shoulders. "I just wanted to tell her where I was, that's all."

"Well you can't be calling her. She's part of your people, places and things, so you might as well forget about her."

I nodded yes, but I knew I'd never forget about Renée, nor would I stop being friends with her. That would be something I'd just have to keep to myself until I was stronger.

Next it was the social worker telling me that I needed to call IBM, because Laney had contacted my doctor wanting to know my medical condition. She also suggested I get honest with Kelisha and tell her that I was in rehab. I couldn't imagine doing either, but after speaking with Dylan and Russell I realized it was the best thing, especially since IBM was paying the bill. I called the job and spoke with Laney, and before I started crying I managed to tell her the truth. She said that she knew I drank a lot but didn't realize that I had a problem with drugs. She said not to worry, because I'd have a job when I returned.

Russell and I were also beginning to deal with issues of our own that had long festered inside, so our rooming together became a problem. We'd go to our room between each session, and since one of the rules was that you couldn't sleep during the day, we used that time to argue.

Those arguments escalated when it came time for me to write my life and drug history. I'd watch Russell sitting at the desk in our room writing and sometimes he'd read his notes aloud and ask me what I thought.

For me, though, it was different—Russell had put a stop to my writing five years before when he'd discovered my journal. Every time I thought about writing, all I had to do was recall him beating me with that sneaker and his threat to kill me if I ever wrote again.

I now wondered, though, if under these circumstances he would make an exception. Rather than ask his permission, I decided to do my writing in another girl's room. But as if he had a built in sensor, Russell found out.

"Why do you keep going in that bitch's room every night?" he asked one afternoon while we were getting ready for dinner.

"Just hangin' out," I answered.

"You sure you ain't fuckin' her?"

"Russell, please."

"Yeah right, Brenda. What, do you think I'm an asshole?"

"Why would you say that?"

"You been writing, haven't you?"

I didn't answer.

"I thought I told you not to fuckin' write."

"But Russell—"

"But, shit. Where is it?"

I thought back to what I'd cautiously written. "It ain't nothing, really."

"Then why you hiding it?"

"Cause I know how you are."

"Git it."

I walked out the room, hurried down the hall into the girl's room and pulled my book from underneath her mattress. I hadn't written very many pages, maybe about ten. Mostly about high school having been where I'd started smoking weed. The one thing I knew he wouldn't like was what I'd written about Michael, my very first boyfriend, who had also dated Lena. Even though Russell was aware of all this I knew he wouldn't like my writing about it.

With my journal in hand I returned to the room where he

was laying across the bed probably trying to figure out how he could pull off beating me without making any noise.

He sat up and snatched the book from my resistant hands. "Give it here."

I stepped backwards until I felt the chair behind me. Once again I found myself watching as he read my journal.

"So, the only man you ever loved was Michael?" he asked.

"What are you talkin' about?"

"Why are you always tryin' to hurt me Brenda?" he asked, having risen from the bed.

"Russell, I'm not trying to hurt you. That was when I was 15 when I was with Michael."

"You know, you really are a ho'. What did you do, fuck all your cousin's men?"

"I never even slept with him then," I said, it being the truth.

"Look, you tell Dylan you don't wanna write."

"But Russell, it's not fair. You're writing. I'm supposed to write too," I said, barely believing I was defending myself.

"The shit you write is fucked up. Bad enough I found that shit about that nigga stickin' his finger in your pussy."

My body tensed up as I prepared myself to be hit.

"You might as well stop that fucken cryin' cause ain't nobody gonna hit your fucked-up ass."

"I'm not fucked up. I'm trying to get better."

"So you gonna write about all the niggas you fucked?" he asked, standing over me and waving the notebook in my face.

"Russell, I didn't fuck a lot of niggas."

"How many times did you fuck Michael, huh Brenda? How many times?"

My body jumped uncontrollably thinking he was about to hit me.

"I don't know what your dumb ass is jumping for."

"Russell, I'm sorry," I said, sick of hearing myself be sorry for things I had or hadn't done, while he took ownership for nothing.

He grabbed me by the face and pulled me up from the chair.

A knock at the door made him release his grip. We both grew quiet.

"Do you want me to get it?" I asked, all the while walking towards the door, relieved that we were being interrupted.

"Go 'head."

On the other side of the door stood one of the members of Russell's group.

"Is everything ok?" he asked.

Russell spoke up from behind me. "Yeah, why?"

"Well, I could hear y'all next door. You sure?" he asked, looking directly at me for an answer.

"No, it's okay."

I closed the door and stood there hoping the interruption had somehow changed Russell's attitude. He patted the space on the bed next to him for me to sit down. Gently, he massaged his hand up and down my thigh.

"You know what you need to do, right?"

I didn't say anything, but I knew the routine. What I didn't know was how long I could go on submitting to him like this. Weren't things supposed to be different now that we were clean?

But nothing was changing, because I didn't know how to get from under his control. My husband, regardless of how he treated me, always needed to be reassured that I still wanted him.

For different reasons our nights began turning out like this, and I felt like he was stopping my growth yet continuing with his. He was writing and doing the things he needed to do, yet telling me that I better not tell anybody our business. He wasn't hitting me, but we were arguing with the threat of my being beaten looming over me and of course afterwards we'd have sex. But I didn't dare complain to anyone.

The next Saturday in women's group the subject was domestic violence. Each woman took a turn describing an abusive relationship, but somehow I didn't think they compared with mine. I figured any one of my stories could outdo theirs, so I shared about getting my collarbone broke in Charlotte. When I finished the counselor asked me if I was still afraid of Russell. I wanted these women to believe I could handle my situation, but when I shook my head no, my tears said yes. They were tears that I couldn't control, sobs that I'd been holding back since the pieces of my life had begun unraveling there at Fairmount.

Dylan was told about my breakdown in women's group and insisted that if I wanted to begin recovering I'd have to move out of the room with Russell. I agreed to the move, knowing that this might be my only chance to have a break from Russell. I also knew that he'd be pissed. When I returned from group that afternoon Russell stormed into the room.

"What's this shit about you wantin' to move to another room?" he asked.

"I didn't say that I wanted to move they asked me."

He stood in front of me, blocking the window. "Well you musta been tellin' 'em somethin'."

I had my head in my hands, hoping he wouldn't hit me. "Russell, everybody has been hearing us arguing. I don't know what to do."

"You tell them that if we have to move to separate rooms then we're leaving."

"We can't leave; we won't be hurtin' nobody but ourselves. Maybe this might help. This way we can concentrate on ourselves."

"That's your problem; all you care about is your fuckin' self."

I turned my head away from him.

"They say if we wanna stay clean we have to follow their suggestions."

"Yeah right. We'll see."

The next day I moved into a room at the other end of the hall, which I shared with another woman. Russell moved into a room on the third floor, sharing it with about four men— something he definitely wasn't used to.

But our counselors didn't stop there. Next we were told not to eat together or sit together during lectures. The goal was for us to interact with other people and become independent of each other. Our treatment teams went even further by moving us to separate buildings. When they saw that we weren't taking it seriously they put us on a restriction so that we were only allowed to spend two hours a day together.

One night after dinner we went for a walk, and as soon as it was dark enough we slipped into the Blue Cruiser and made love in the backseat that was wide enough to hold a full size bed. Two days later we were confronted in our groups. I tried to tell my group that Russell had forced me. But Dylan approached me with a question I'd never considered.

"How long are you gonna keep blaming everything on Russell?"

I was totally shocked. Up until then everything *was* Russell's fault. I was his victim, or so I thought. But through group I found out differently. I was both a victim and an active participant. Was it his fault that every time he hurt me I'd lash out by being with another man? Had it been his fault that I kept coming back to him after he'd abused me so viciously? Was it his fault that I'd deceived my cousin, and that my relationship with Russell caused her to have a nervous breakdown? And was it his fault that I'd had an abortion?

My parents and Kelisha were my first and only visitors. That was the day that I explained to my daughter why I was in Fairmount and why I'd lied to her. She understood and was happy that I was trying to get better and even happier that I hadn't gone to Florida without her.

On another day Eve came with Rusty, whom I took to feed the horses after he and Russell played baseball. He didn't require much of an explanation because he was so young. It still hurt for our families to see us like this, but we all knew it was for the best.

My family's second visit wasn't as easy, because it was combined with a family session with my treatment team. It was heart-wrenching to hear my parents and Kelisha talk about what I'd put them through. My mother's main concern was how I was always breaking promises to Kelisha. She said I'd always been a habitual liar. It all started when I was young—I would lie about where I was going, what I was doing and whom I was with. I had lied about everything. My marriage with Russell, my drug use, and my ability to be a mother and wife had all been built on lies.

Then my Dad spoke up about how he'd tried to protect me and how I'd resisted that protection. I believed I had a better relationship with him simply because he was the one who spoiled me while my mother was the disciplinarian. Even with all that he gave me, I still wanted to do things my way. I always believed that neither of them knew what they were talking about, that they were old-fashioned. Now I wished *I* could be that old-fashioned. But as if hearing from them wasn't enough, my team also wanted to hear from Kelisha.

"I'd like to like to ask your daughter some questions if that's okay."

I nodded yes, but in my head I shouted no because I was too afraid of what she would say. I was too afraid that she might voice something she'd seen or heard that would not only hurt me but my parents as well.

"Kelisha, is that okay with you?"

She looked at La-La and said, "yes."

"When you think back about, let's say a month ago? Why don't you tell me what you noticed about your Mom and Dad?"

"Uhm—" she turned her eyes towards me to see if it was okay to talk.

I nodded my head for her to go on.

"Well, Daddy was always telling us not to tell anybody what went on in our house," she said, her pony tails swinging as she rocked back and forth in the chair.

"And what did you see going on?"

She shrugged her shoulders.

The room was quiet; I was sitting on my hands.

"Just all the stuff they were doing and all the company."

"How did you feel about that?"

She smiled. I assumed she was remembering. "I don't know. I like all the stuff they get me."

"What do you get Kelisha?"

"They buy lots of toys and dolls and stuff for me and my little brother."

"Anything you don't like?"

"I don't like the way Daddy hollers at us all the time when

we're not doing anything wrong."

"Anything else?"

"He took us down North Philly one time and they were shooting over the car."

My mother shot a look at me that cut me down further than anything anyone could ever say. I knew she'd never forgive me for putting Kelisha in such danger.

"So if you could have one thing from your mom and dad what would that be?"

"I like living with my La-La and Pop-Pop, but I want to come live with them."

"And Brenda, what do you say to that?"

I couldn't say anything because I was crying too hard at the stark reality that I hadn't been a good mother to my children, or a good daughter to my parents.

chapter fourteen

Money Pit
Summer, 1987

Armed with 40 days of recovery, we left Fairmount Institute on a sunny April afternoon to begin our new lives. It had been suggested that we attend 90 meetings in 90 days, and stay away from people, places and things that were connected to our addiction. The staff also thought it was a good idea that we attend our meetings separately, allowing us to focus on our individual recovery. The most insightful thing they said was that since Russell and I had spent our entire relationship getting high, that we really didn't know each other now that we were drug-free, so we shouldn't be surprised if we woke up one morning and wondered what the hell we were doing together.

Our first stop once we reached West Philly was to pick up Rusty from day care. We pulled up to the church at 57th and Vine and observed him from the doorway until he spun around, saw us and jumped into my arms. I began crying and kissing his little yellow face as I smothered him with affection. I passed him to Russell, who hugged him some more. There was no need to explain to the teachers who we were, because they could tell.

We then headed north on I-95 out to Holmesburg to see my parents and Kelisha. La-La and Pop-Pop were overjoyed to have us home and kept telling us how healthy we looked.

Russell gave them a plaque he'd made in occupational therapy, which read, "What you do is God's gift to you. What you make of yourself is your gift to God."

When Kelisha walked in from school she was surprised to find us sitting at the dining room table. We hugged and kissed her, and I realized how much I'd missed my children.

We took the children to Sizzlers on Roosevelt Boulevard for dinner, where we listened to them rattling on about what they'd been doing. We'd missed Kelisha's spring music concert at school and Rusty was talking so much that he lost his voice and we had to show him how to clear his throat as he kept trying to repeat the word "hello." He also had a fashion show coming up in which he wanted Russell to participate.

Their most pressing question was when they could come home. We told them that as soon as we "got things together," but definitely by the end of the school year.

Later that evening after we returned the children to their respective homes, we headed downtown to the Wanamaker House. After parking, we checked the mailbox, which was overflowing with bills, my paychecks and Russell's Worker's Compensation that had been piling up. We had over $3000 in checks and owed more than that in bills. We talked about our finances and decided that we definitely had to move.

Upon entering our apartment the first thing I noticed was how clean it was, which wasn't how I'd left it. On the kitchen counter I found an envelope. In it was a note saying that management was charging us $50 for maid service. We'd left food and dirty dishes, and when the smell became unbearable the neighbors reported it to the office. Imagine old fish sitting out for over a month.

Our first night home was pretty mellow. There were a few phone calls but mostly we were just happy to be together. More importantly, it was the first time in 10 years that we made love without being under the influence.

Two days later I returned to work, nervous about how I looked, what people thought and how my coworkers would receive me. While at Fairmount I'd worn jeans and sweatshirts everyday. I'd been sure to go shopping before my first day back and wore a red silk dress and matching red pumps, the soft silk making me feel like lady again.

As I walked off the elevator and onto the 7th floor, I spoke to everyone as if I'd been there yesterday. Laney, who'd been my manager since I'd started at IBM in 1984, greeted me in front of her office with a hug.

"Laney, thank you for not telling anyone," I said as she closed the door behind us.

"I would never do that, Brenda. Plus it's against policy. But I am curious as to what happened."

I shrugged my shoulders and said "I don't know we just . . . were . . . you know getting high socially, hanging out and stuff and it got out of control for the both of us."

"I know a lot of people go out for happy hour but was it more than just drinking? Was it drugs too?" she asked leaning forward across her desk.

My face got hot and my eyes began swelling with tears. I didn't want to break down but this was a tough spot to be in. I wondered just how much she was entitled to know. I didn't want to jeopardize my job anymore than I already had.

"Laney, it was a little bit of everything but it got out of control and I wanted to get some help so I called the EAP people before I lost my job."

"Brenda I didn't know it was that bad. I don't want you to worry about that or anything else, because you can come in here, close the door and confide in me anytime you want."

I nodded my head, realizing that she was being sincere, because this woman had helped me many times with job opportunities and when I'd come to her with problems.

"Brenda, I'm just glad you recognized that you had a problem and you and your husband were able to get help."

"Thanks Laney."

"Now what I do need to tell you is that it's IBM policy that if at anytime management thinks you're getting high again, we have the right to ask you to go across the street to the doctor, and if tested positive, you will immediately be terminated."

"I understand," I said, feeling scared for the first time that I could lose my job.

After further discussion of what my responsibilities would be and whom I'd be supporting, I went to my desk. Everything was the same and nobody appeared to be looking at me differently, so it was probably my insecurities that made me feel watched. Sitting at my desk I tried to figure out where to start. The first time the phone rang I feared it would be someone on the other end asking for coke, reefer or maybe money I owed them.

The other difficulty I had was going to the bathroom. I'd done so many drugs in the ladies room during working hours—sitting on the toilet, flushing it while I took a hit, rolling a joint to smoke at lunch or splitting a package for sale—that I avoided going until I went home because I couldn't stand the way the room made my heart pound. All of this made me glad to know that our offices would be moving from 17th and Market Streets to Commerce Square at 21st and Market. I so badly needed a new work environment.

I didn't bother to discuss what had happened with any of my co-workers. However, I did notice the change in people's attitude towards me. Since they'd been seen socializing with me that they might be viewed as having done the same things I'd been doing, which in most cases was true. People who'd been to my house for parties, who had hung in the bars with me after work, and even those I'd sold drugs to barely spoke to me. I guess they felt that if they'd hung out with me, then they, too, could end up in rehab.

My performance at work improved since I didn't have drugs to distract me. Laney began telling me what a good job I was doing, clearly implying that they'd expected me to screw up, but I covered my butt with everything I did. Anytime I finished something I checked it multiple times to make sure it was flawless. I was also sure not to be late for work or miss a day.

At home we were still getting the children on the weekends, but now our time was spent differently. We visited museums, parks and the playground. IBM had their family picnic at Indian Springs and we went as a family without getting into an argument. This was unusual, especially when Russell saw the brother he'd sworn I'd slept with during one of my trips to Atlanta. I didn't even know the man but I did know it wasn't easy for Russell. I was grateful he was making an effort.

Having done the math on the bills against the legitimate money we had coming in, we began house hunting, eventually renting a three bedroom house located at 52nd and Media Streets in West Philly. 1447 N. 52nd Street was an old wood-frame house, with lime-green stucco, a cement slab for a backyard and no modern amenities. The big difference, though, was the rent: only $250 a month vs. the $850 we paid for our 18th-floor studio.

The immediate neighborhood consisted of two bars in a one-block radius—one on the corner of Media Street and the other on Lancaster Avenue. On the right side of us was a vacant lot and next to it a building that was often rented out for parties on Saturdays and church on Sundays. The closest playground was across the street, which was covered with broken beer bottles.

It was more than that. It was the fact that we were going to be living in the ghetto—the hood—and even though Russell had grown up in that environment, I didn't want it for me and definitely didn't want it for my children. My complaints were met with the argument that I thought I was too good to live on 52nd Street, that I'd been spoiled by growing up in the Northeast. Actually, I didn't see what was so wrong with wanting a better environment for my children. I eventually gave in, because I'd been learning that I had to humble myself, and what could be more humbling than living on 52nd Street?

By now everybody we'd gotten high with was smoking crack, including our siblings. Russell and I had to step back from offering our help, because it was impossible to force anyone into treatment or to admit they had a problem. All we could do was stay clean, stick together and be an example.

But we could feel people change; they backed away from us. Even Eve distanced herself, because we no longer got high together. We also no longer took drugs to Tank in jail. But as good as I felt believing that maybe now Russell and I had a chance, I secretly missed the excitement of our lifestyle.

My parents and I were now able to talk about addiction and recovery. They often asked me if they'd gone wrong somewhere. I kept telling them they raised us well; they'd taught us about morals, respect, responsibility and hard work, but we'd made our choices. I explained that it wasn't something they did or didn't do, that addiction was a disease. I knew that the only way I could take away the hurt I'd given them was to stay clean. And because that was all they were asking of me, I had to do my best to stick with it.

It was my sister Gwennie who was fighting to get off drugs. She'd been going to church but said she felt like she needed something more. It was during one of these conversations that I was able to make some suggestions.

"Sis, I need you to give me some advice on how to stop getting high. I mean I've been going to church and praying, but it's like I just need something else."

"Gwennie I can't tell you what to do, but I can tell you that going to NA meetings does help because you're around people who understand what you're going through and you can talk about it."

"I talk about with my girfriends."

"But they all get high. They're just listening and passing the coke at the same time."

"So what are you saying?"

"You need new people, places and things to be around, you can't stay clean in an environment filled with drugs and people that do them. You notice that I don't hang out with the same people anymore, right?"

"Yeah, you're right. So you think I should go to a meeting with you?"

"Absolutely. I'll pick you up this weekend."

I took my sister to a meeting that weekend, and she became more involved than I ever did—she totally absorbed everything about Narcotics Anonymous, and was well known throughout the Tri State Area until she died in 1996. On the day she was buried, the church was filled to standing room only with people honoring her.

But it was some of the smaller things I noticed about recovery that I enjoyed. I was no longer gritting my teeth and complaining to the dentist that they were sensitive. My clothes didn't get thrown around at night, so they didn't have to be dry cleaned so many times. My pantyhose lasted longer and my thinking was a little clearer. The coolest thing was that I was actually learning the correct words to songs.

Yes, life was good. But life was also fooling me into thinking it would stay that way, because it was becoming obvious that Russell and I were growing in two separate directions.

chapter fifteen

Motherhood Challenges
1987

This is the way it was supposed to be—no arguments, no fighting and nobody knocking on our door looking to get high. We were a family. However, needing something to fill an obvious void for excitement, we chose dog breeding.

We'd had Bear since 1982, when Russell purchased him for Kelisha. Since then he'd traveled with us everywhere we'd lived. Russell, however, decided that in order to keep Bear from humping on everything, we'd get him a mate. Chia was a furry white Chow-Chow who became pregnant shortly after we purchased her. At first we gave away the puppies to family and friends until Russell had the bright idea that we could make money by turning our house into a kennel. Not only did Bear impregnate Chia, but when his female offspring were old enough they, too, would have puppies. Needless to say, our house couldn't accommodate such a brood. There'd be a litter of puppies in the corner of the living room, where our black carpet was now stained from poop, not to mention the smell of poop mixed with the Lysol we used to clean it up. There'd also be a litter that had to be bottle-fed in our bedroom and another in Kelisha's room, all needing attention.

Before we made money in our new venture there were expenses: shots, pounds of dog food, trips to the Vet and official papers to be ordered. But what selling Chow-Chows gave us was the sense of hustling. People were calling the house to inquire; Russell was going out to exchange money for dogs, so we were still in the game but with a different product—one that eventually became more of a source of contention between us than anything else. Dogs, however, weren't the only pets we had.

Rusty's grandmother, Gloria, had brought him a bird. One day when we'd all gone out we forgot to close the door to the bedroom where it was caged. Returning home later, we were greeted at the front door by Bear, who had a mouth full of bird feathers. Russell ran upstairs only to find birdseed strewn about the floor, a mangled birdcage and a few feathers, but no bird. We told Rusty that we'd left a window open and it had flown away, as neither of us had the heart to tell him that the bird had been Bear's supper.

Then there were Kelisha's fish, which were also kept in her room. For some reason I thought the fish were cold and told Kelisha to turn up the heat in the tank to warm them. In a few hours the poor fish had cooked.

The worst of all those animals were the mice, which came from the trash strewn lot next door. No amount of rat poison kept them away. We learned to exist with them by cleaning up mice turds every morning from the stove and countertop before cooking breakfast.

But as much as I detested living on 52nd Street there were fun times also, like vacations to Ocean City, Maryland and summer camp for the kids when Toya came to visit. We'd even gone to my mother's family reunion in Richmond with a side trip to Kings Dominion.

We'd fly kites with the kids, have barbecues in the cement yard and picnics in the park, and Russell would play catch with Rusty at the playground. The children's favorite game was "putting on the hits," where we'd each dress up and take turns singing and dancing to our own tunes. It was our version of karaoke, and Russell had all the musical equipment. Even though none of us could sing it always drew a good laugh, especially when Russell would put on my heels and dress and sing to Whitney Houston.

Rusty, who was now six, had become more than just a stepson to me, filling a lot of special places in my heart. One evening he and Kelisha were cleaning up the kitchen, and I heard a blood-curdling scream. I rushed downstairs and saw that he'd fallen off a chair while trying to clean out the sink for his sister. Rusty was trying his best not to cry while telling me that his ankle only hurt a little bit. I sat him down in the living room, propped up his leg, packed it with ice and resumed putting away laundry.

Later that night Kelisha called me to her room to tell me that Rusty was still complaining and wouldn't stop crying. This wasn't like him—he didn't cry unless something was really bothering him. That tipped me off that he was in serious pain. Kelisha kept saying that it was probably broken because he couldn't move it, and I kept saying it was probably sprained. Realizing the pain that he was in, I called 911 and had them send a police car to take us to Children's Hospital. After an examination by the doctor and an x-ray, we learned that Rusty's ankle was broken, and they fitted him for a cast and crutches.

I'd left a message for Russell on the machine at home and another with Eve to let him know to pick us up at the hospital. He was unreachable because he was at a meeting. When he finally arrived at 1:00 a.m., we both had an attitude.

"Russell where have you been?" I asked, tired and pissed off.

"You know I was at a meeting," he said, pulling out of the parking lot on 34th Street.

"Till one o'clock in the morning?"

"I had a business meeting to go to."

"That's bullshit, every time I need you you're at a damn meeting."

In between our bickering the kids were trying to tell him what happened.

"I'm doing what my sponsor suggests and that's make meetings."

"Yeah, but what about us?"

"You a woman—you act like you can't handle shit."

"I understand, but you don't see me spending all my time at meetings."

"Well that's on you, maybe you wanna get high."

I felt myself cringing every time he turned to look at me, fearing he might hit me for speaking up. He recognized that and shouted, "I don't know why the fuck you keep jumping, ain't nobody gonna hit your dumb ass."

The children now sat quietly in the back seat.

Rusty's next visit to the hospital was when he came down with what appeared to be a cold. I stayed home for a few days to care for him, but he wasn't getting better. The pediatrician suggested Tylenol but advised me that if I noticed any signs of dehydration I should take him to the emergency room. I went upstairs to check on Rusty and could tell he was worse. I checked his temperature; it was 106°. His little body was on fire, his lips cracked and dry. He was dehydrated. I called Russell and told him we needed to take him to Children's Hospital where my son cried in my arms as they fed him intravenously to bring back his body fluids.

I always made it a point to keep Rusty's mother's family abreast of anything that went on with him. His grandmother was very much a part of his life, and he often spent time with them. Sandy, his mother, who was still living in Ohio, called one afternoon to check on her son. I could tell she was a little intoxicated, but it was never my intention to keep them apart, and since going to rehab I'd learned that my addiction was no better than hers. A few minutes later Kelisha began calling me.

"Mom, can you come up here? Rusty's crying, something's wrong."

"What's wrong sweetheart?" I asked as he sat on the side of the tub where he'd been taking a bath.

"Sandy told me that I can't call you Mommy anymore, because she's my mommy," he managed to say through sniffles.

I didn't have time to think about how I felt because I had to console him. I took him out of the tub, put his underwear on and carried him downstairs to tell Russell what happened.

"You don't have to listen to that shit. Sandy is crazy," Russell told his son.

I sat Rusty on my lap because I knew he needed to hear more than that.

"Baby, you don't have to stop calling me mommy unless you want to. I know that I'm not your mom, that Sandy is. You know that too, right?"

He nodded his head yes.

"I'm not trying to take her place, but I want to be your other mom who can do the things your real mom can't do right now, until she gets better. You know I love you very much and that I love taking care of you. You remember when I came to Ohio to get you right?"

"Yes."

"Well, your mom wanted me to come so I could help her. And remember all the kisses and hugs we share and all those times you were sick and hurt yourself that I took care of you and all the fun things we do? Well, none of that will ever stop, okay?"

He nodded again, this time with a big smile.

I gave him a big squeeze and a kiss.

"Now go upstairs and get dressed," I said as he jumped out of my lap.

He paused midway up the steps. "Mom, can I still call you mom?"

"Yes, as much as you want."

Kelisha was now 11 and in the 6th grade and had grown into a beautiful little girl. She was long and lean like her parents, with golden brown skin and a head full of long ponytails. At an early age she wore the best designer clothes—I'm sure they made her stand out among her peers, but she'd never been a show off. She was enjoying living with us and attending Shoemaker Junior High at 53rd and Media Streets. It was only a block away and she picked up Rusty from Hesston Elementary to walk home together.

After a few months, I'd begun noticing changes in her schoolwork. Her grades were dropping and I couldn't understand why, because both Russell and I helped with homework and she studied for tests. I did know that living and going to school in West Philly was a different environment for her both socially and academically her school in because the Northeast had been predominately White and now she was in a majority Black junior high school.

When I spoke with her teacher, he proceeded to tell me that Kelisha was associating with a group of girls who were a bad influence. He told me how some of the girls were intimidating her, throwing her books out of the window, and telling her she acted like a white girl. It was obvious to him that Kelisha was a good kid and he wished he had more kids like her. When I asked him if he thought Kelisha needed to be in another school, though, he said no and that perhaps talking to her might help.

I talked to Kelisha and told her that she didn't need to try to be like the other girls, that she should be herself, even though I knew the peer pressure was hard. Russell also talked to her and told her that if anybody fucked with her to let him know and he'd fuck somebody up. Our responses were so different when it came to giving the children values, maybe he was so harsh because he was being overprotective and didn't know how to show his concern.

A few weeks later, while cleaning the living room, I decided to look through her book bag and check her home-work. She wasn't failing, but her grades still hadn't improved, and it wasn't so much the subject matter she wasn't grasping but her behavior that had become a problem.

When I was about to close her notebook, I found a piece of paper that read; "Kelisha and William sitting in a tree, f-u-c-k-i-n-g."I was stunned. I couldn't believe my daughter had done this. What had happened? The mere thought of her being sexually active frightened me. She didn't even have her period yet. I called Russell downstairs and showed him what I'd found. The kids were upstairs so they didn't hear his reaction.

"Get her the fuck outta here and send her back to your mother's. I'm not having this shit. "He then stormed out of the house to a meeting. I was crushed. How could he cut off his daughter so easily?

Once again, without taking the time for a real discussion or thinking it through on my own, I allowed Russell to make the decision. I called my parents, his mother and my sponsor and cried to them all. My parents immediately told me to send her back to them. They said it wasn't worth taking the chance of something happening to her at school or the possibility of Russell being angry enough to hit her.

My thought wasn't so much that Russell would harm her as much as my failure as a mother. In rehab it had taken me quite some time to identify with women who openly admitted that they'd they neglected their children. To me that always meant you left them unattended, that you didn't properly feed or clothe them. As I'd moved through this thing called recovery, however, it began to be revealed that yes, I had abandoned my children. I'd neglected them plenty of times, allowing Kelisha to live with my parents and Rusty to live with Eve because of my lifestyle. Thank God our parents stepped in to take care of the kids when they did.

Before I went upstairs to break the news that she'd be returning to my parents, I sat on the couch and listened to her and Rusty upstairs jumping up and down on my bed. I said the serenity prayer and walked up the steps.

"I need to talk to you two," I said from the doorway.

"What's wrong Mom?" asked Rusty.

"Kelisha, I found this in your book bag," I said, holding up the sheet of paper.

Her eyes got big and full of tears, "Mom, I didn't do it, them girls at school did it!"

"Well, Daddy and I decided that since you're having problems with your grades and those girls are bothering you, we think it'll be better if you go back to stay with La-La until school is out."

"But Mom, I want to stay here with you and Rusty," she pleaded.

"Oh Kiz," I said, reaching out to hug both of them. "We're gonna still be together, but I don't want anybody bothering you."

"I won't let nobody bother her, Mom," Rusty said proudly.

"But whose gonna get Rusty from school?" she asked.

I couldn't answer, because I wasn't sure how to respond to their immediate concern for each other. Maybe I had done something right.

"Am I still gonna get to come home on the weekends?"

"Do I have to leave, too?" Rusty asked.

Rather than answer I pulled the two of them to me and we fell across the bed—the two of them landing on me in a big hug.

chapter sixteen

Superwoman
1988

Within a year I discovered there was a flip side to my new-found lifestyle, and the first thing I noticed was how I was totally unable to manage our finances. I'd never been good at paying bills and had never accumulated much of a savings, and it was worse now that I didn't have any extra cash. My checking account was an easy example, as I was writing checks and trying to make it to the bank before they cashed, resulting in bounced checks and a negative balance.

We had enormous utility bills trying to keep that old house warm in the winter, and since neither of us wanted to be broke we had a hard time sharing our money, nothing was paid on time. There were bills piling up on our kitchen table from our years of reckless living, and my credit cards had been maxed out years ago. We'd accumulated a stack of parking tickets while living in center city which resulted in a $600 bill for the removal of an orange boot that had been put on the Blue Cruiser. To put it simply, we were in debt because we weren't used to paying bills on a monthly basis—probably because we'd never lived anywhere long enough to learn any consistency.

I made a good salary at IBM, in addition to my overtime pay, but I'd picked up a new addiction—shopping. When I didn't have the cash I'd borrow my father's credit cards and pay him back in monthly installments. I'd shop for the children, pick up things for Russell and buy items for the house. This behavior reminded me of my addiction, of the ways I used to hide cocaine from Russell. It was the mere rush I received from buying things that I enjoyed the most. This time, though, I was shopping at the boutiques in center city and hiding my clothing purchases. Anytime there was tension between my husband and me, I'd leave the house and head to the store.

I realized my spending was out of control following one argument, when I'd gone to the grocery store and spent $300 on groceries we already had. When it was over, we had two turkeys in the refrigerator and three gallons of ice cream.

Russell decided he'd had enough when one evening he went to Super Fresh in Ardmore to cash his paycheck and they deducted $200 for a check I'd bounced.

We thought the way to fix our financial problems was to file for bankruptcy, which we did, hoping that it would give us a fresh start. With that done, Russell wanted us to buy a house. I wasn't so sure we were ready to take that step, because our marriage was still as fragile as our recovery, but I went along with the plan. First we approached my mother and her sisters to arrange a personal sale of Nanny's house, but they didn't trust our finances. Then we made a great attempt at buying the house we were living in. We actually made it all the way to the settlement table, but the seller's paperwork was questionable so we had to back out.

Russell's way of coping with all of this was to increase his attendance at NA meetings and social events. Someone was always calling the house for him to attend parties and business meetings where he'd taken on some responsibility. Rarely did we attend anything as a couple, with the exception of the Regional NA Convention. I found it to be overwhelming, while Russell, because of the social butterfly he'd become, could barely stay in the room we'd rented for the weekend.

I didn't complain, because I was confused about how I was feeling about my life in general and I relished any time I had to myself. To me even though we were supposed to have these individual lives, I was still allowing Russell to control mine. When my girlfriend Neicy's mother died, Russell didn't think it was a good idea for me to show my condolences by attending the funeral, because she still got high. I'd have to talk to Renée when he wasn't home for the same reason. I knew he meant well, but these were real friends I wasn't willing to give up just because we no longer shared the same vices. These women had been in my life for a long time and were part of my support structure, regardless of what I did.

Russell, though, never included Eve in that category. Surely she was still getting high, and so I resented my husband, but that was only the beginning.

My interest in sex had also waned. Most times I just went through the motions, lacking the aggressiveness or creativity I had when I used to get high. Russell noticed this and thought having another child might put a spark into our marriage. Every month when my period came on brought another disappointment and an argument that the fault was with me for having that abortion. My fear was that Russell would go out and make a baby elsewhere.

I believe we both wanted to make our marriage work, so we agreed to get counseling. It may have helped, but after only a few sessions Russell became paranoid and thought the counselor wanted to have sex with me. The only insight we gained in that short time was when the counselor explained what our marriage was missing, chaos. He believed that without all the madness that used to make up our relationship, we didn't think we had one. That was something we both agreed on.

But there were spurts of light under the dark shroud. My husband surprised me by showing up at my office one afternoon and presenting me with a new diamond wedding ring. He was also known for sending flowers on a weekly basis.

To his credit, Russell had been making some headway with his education by attending school two nights a week to get his diploma, and he eventually graduated from Community College. That night we all went to dinner and I presented him with a framed poem I had written. He was a bit emotional that his success had meant so much to me, but what he didn't under-stand was that my urge to write had become so overwhelming that I was simply using him as an outlet.

My obsession with writing had begun at J.H. Brown Elementary School. Nightly I'd listen to the radio and write down the lyrics to songs or try to make up my own. My sister Gwennie had given me my first diary and that was when I began making journal entries and writing poems. I loved reading, and remember the early versions of *Madeline, The Bobsey Twins* and *Nancy Drew*. As I got older there were magazines: *True Confessions* and *Seventeen*.

When I was about 13, I made an important discovery while rummaging through the bottom of my father's closet. I came across a ragged and yellowed paperback, *Mandingo* by Kyle Onstott; it was here that even though fictionalized I read about the torture of slaves. One story in particular told of a man having his penis nailed to a log while the rest of his body was set on fire. Horrified though I was, I wanted to know more about my heritage and so began to read Nikki Giovanni, Sonia Sanchez, Amira Baraka (a.k.a. Leroi Jones), Don L. Lee and June Jordan.

By high school I didn't go anywhere without a notebook to write poems or anything that came into my head. My parents subscribed to *Ebony* and *Jet* and our neighbor subscribed to Philly's black newspaper, *The Philadelphia Tribune*. It was good to know that I no longer had to rely on white magazines to make a woman out of me—especially after the excitement of discovering my first copy of *Essence* in my sister's basement.

It was these publications that kept me current about what was going on in black America, especially since the area where I lived and went to school was lily-white. School, though, was where I began to wreak havoc on my white counterparts. During my years in high school I had no problem walking the halls of Lincoln High School, my afro in check, telling white students (crackers, honkeys and whatever term was popular at the time) that I hated them and why. If they weren't aware of what their ancestors had done, then I made myself responsible to tell them.

The next book that impacted me was *Soledad Brother*. The passion between the imprisoned radical George Jackson and Angela Davis was more than a teenager could handle, and it was all on paper. I went from the Panthers to Islam and everything in between.

Somewhere in the last 10 years, however, I'd lost that woman who wanted to be the next leader of her people. There were no more poems about saving my race and certainly no more love poems. Now all I had were the notes I'd write at work and throw in the trash at the end of the day, because there was no way I'd ever let Russell see another thing I'd written or let him know that our marriage was choking the life out of me.

Then, denying it even to myself, I began experiencing flashbacks from the abuse I'd suffered in my relationship with Russell. I didn't dare mention them to him and wasn't even sure why it was happening. The first time was one day while I was at work when the memory of one of his episodes exploded in my head causing me to get dizzy.

Without wanting to I'd recall the short time when we lived on Bustleton Avenue and me and Kelisha had come home to discover that he'd removed our queen sized bed simply because he'd wanted to prove to Lena that we didn't live together. There'd also been the time he'd beat me in front of his mother while she sat watching a boxing match on television until she said, "I think that's enough Russell."

I cursed myself for not following through the time after one of his beatings when I'd called a shelter but was too scared to leave the house. How had he imbedded that kind of fear? How had he found my weakness? Individually, these things may not have been awful, but all together they had hurt and humiliated me.

But that was only the beginning. Even during the supposed good times my mind would focus on the past. I tried to turn it off, because I felt stupid for having stayed with a man who beat me, for believing each and every time that he'd changed. I hated myself for thinking I had no choice, for trying to be part of a family that despised me. What was worse was that I found it made me hate *myself* more than I hated *him*.

He'd accused me of having sex with so many men that I'd even begun to doubt myself. The only time I'd been a whore was for him, and all those wild sexual fantasies that I'd participated in so I could get high and drown out my feelings. I'd been his sex slave, and now I detested it when he touched me. I'd learned that I'd minimized the times he'd repeatedly raped me, always saying to myself that "he just took some pussy." But what about when I didn't *want* to give myself to him?

I even went as far as hating my brothers for not saving me from Russell. Even if I'd gone back a million times, he should've gotten his ass kicked at least once. He should've been made to feel every pain, hit, slap and beat down that I'd felt. Would he have been man enough for that? If they had simply had him killed I'd be in a better place. I was sick of the thought that I'd never fought back, never even lifted a finger to defend myself. I'd just let that man who supposedly loved me beat me down like I was some kind of slave.

Now when I looked at my husband I wanted him dead—I would imagine beating him with the ferocity that he'd beaten me, listening to him beg for me to stop. Who was I fooling? This man didn't love me and I didn't love him.

I kept telling myself that things were different now that we were clean; he didn't beat me anymore, and he wasn't the same person. Yet, I still held a fear of him that I tried to convince myself didn't exist. When we'd argue, he'd often throw things, slam doors and get in my face. Once he even kicked in the bathroom door while the kids were in there because he was angry. When Russell would misplace something he'd always find someone to blame. On time he thought Kelisha had taken a cassette tape and he had harassed her, screaming and cursing, tearing the house up, only to apologize the next day when he found out that his sister had the tape.

It was scary what we were going through, especially since I didn't have a crutch to hang onto. I wanted to get high so badly that I imagined what it would be like, imagined the euphoria I would feel, but I also knew that getting high would be a disappointment to me, my children and my parents. There had to be some other way to get past these feelings.

I desperately needed my husband's attention to fight off these thoughts, but all I received was verbal abuse. He criticized every aspect of my life. It was rare for him to tell me I looked good, smelled good or had done anything well. If I wore perfume, he'd tell me it was too strong and that I must be getting dressed up for someone at work. But it was him that was never home.

I confronted Russell about his constant absence and the fact that I had to do everything around the house. Most times I'd get home from work and Rusty would be outside playing while Russell would be in the house listening to music and talking on the phone. I would often cook dinner in my work clothes while he was upstairs taking a shower, shaving, putting on cologne and getting fresh to go to a meeting. After he'd leave, I'd clean up and help Rusty with his homework before putting him to bed.

The arguments between us began building until one night I didn't think he'd come home at all. When I realized that he hadn't called me during the day to say he had something to do after work, I didn't know what to think. My worst fear was that he was out getting high. I didn't want to panic and call hospitals and police stations, so I called Eve, who claimed she had not heard from him either.

It was 2:00 a.m. when Russell came in. I was still awake watching television, which I'd been doing a lot. His excuse was that he'd gone to a co-worker's house for dinner and to watch movies. I asked him why he hadn't called, and he said he didn't feel like arguing. This pattern became one he repeated.

The head to this thing bubbled over one night when Russell came in late.

"Where you been?" I asked from where I stood, wiping down the washer and dryer that was housed in the overcrowded kitchen.

"I was out! Look, we need to talk."

I stopped what I was doing and faced him. "Alright."

"Neither one of us likes the way things are, and I'm tired of arguing so I'm gonna move out."

I couldn't speak for a second; my emotions were caught between surprise and relief. After all the times that I'd wanted to leave in the past, now he was choosing to leave me.

"Where are you gonna go?"

"My mother's."

"And what am I supposed to do?"

"You'll be alright. I'm gonna help you with the bills. I just need some time to think."

"When is all this gonna happen?"

"Soon."

I remained downstairs late that night, withdrawn in my own world, trying to imagine what my life would be like without him. What kind of things would I do? I couldn't even remember what kinds of things I'd wanted to do. I knew that without him I could write and not worry about him reading and analyzing what I'd written. Maybe I'd even write my book. I'd keep my house clean, go to church, get involved in NA, spend quality time with the children and pay more attention to my health and appearance. Just thinking of being on my own was strange and exciting.

He never left.

Then one night Russell was supposed to pick me up after I'd worked until 9:30 p.m. It wasn't safe to take the 10 trolley home that late at night, but he never called or showed up. I became enraged, took a cab home and began packing. When he got home I told him I was going to stay with my mother until we could learn how to communicate.

While at my parents I tried to make sense out of what was happening. I knew that eventually if things didn't change I would leave for good; I didn't know when or how. When I thought about a permanent separation I wondered what the kids would think and how I would explain it to them. Would he want them on the weekends? Would he want the car? When would I pack? How would I leave? Would he try to keep Rusty?

I grabbed for my spirituality because I felt it was the only thing that could save us. I returned to church and read the Bible. It told me that if I put my faith in God and repented, things would change. In doing this I became friends with Gail, who was a born again Christian. She, too, encouraged me that through Christ my husband and I could make it. Russell even agreed to attend a few of the couple's Christian sessions, but being uninterested he fell asleep. What I learned, though, was that God wouldn't want me to be in a relationship where I had fear of my partner. I even went as far as attending a Christian retreat, but the more I read the Bible, went to church and attended NA meetings, the more confused I became.

Not knowing what to do and feeling guilty, I returned home to Russell.

It was a Monday night when I again questioned Russell about his comings and goings. He was getting dressed to go to a meeting.

"Don't you think you could stay home tonight?"

"Brenda, don't start your shit. You know I have a commitment at this meeting."

"You have a commitment to your family, too. What about that?"

"I take care of my family."

"How can you say that when you're always off with your friends at damn NA meetings?"

"What you need to do is start talking to some women who are married, so you can see how this thing works," he said, referring to the fact that my sponsor was a single woman.

"And that's gonna help me understand why my husband never wants to be at home?"

"What do you want me to do Brenda, move out?"

His comment about moving startled me, because that seemed a bit drastic. Hell I hadn't gone through all those years of hell to give up now that we were drug-free. Instead I decided maybe he was right and made a phone call to a woman who I knew was married.

"Who you talkin' to?" Russell asked when he came in from getting his hairbrush out the car and found me chatting on the phone with a girlfriend.

I covered the phone with my hand. "Yvonne, Marshall's wife," I told him, hoping he'd be pleased that I'd taken his advice.

He went upstairs without responding either way. After a few minutes I hung up the phone and found him sitting on the side of the bed, rubbing lotion into his hands.

"Why you wait 'til I left out to get on the phone?" he asked, admiring himself in the mirror.

I shrugged my shoulders and thought to myself, "*What kind of ridiculous question was that?*"

"You better not be telling her any of my business."

Now I was confused. Hadn't it been him, less than an hour ago, who'd told me to talk to other women? How the hell was I supposed to work out what I was going through if I didn't talk about it?

"Russell, I thought you wanted me to—" I started to say, but he cut me off.

"Yeah well, what were you talkin' about?" He was standing in front of the mirror brushing his hair.

"Do I have to tell you everything?"

"I asked you what you said to her!" he said, his voice now louder.

"Russell, that ain't none of your business," I stated, walking out the bedroom.

"Bitch," I heard him mumble.

"Fuck you!" I replied.

I returned to the kitchen where I'd begun cooking dinner. Rusty was seated at the table doing his homework. The next thing I knew Russell was charging down the steps, backing me up so close to the stove that the gray swoosh on his red and black nylon track suit danced in front of my eyes. Our son took cover and ran into the living room.

"Who the fuck you think you talkin' to?" he asked, wagging his finger in my face.

I knew what was coming and prayed I'd have enough courage to reach behind me and scald him with the pot of rice I was boiling.

"What? I—"

"Brenda, you don't fuckin' talk to me like that! I don't know what that bitch told you, but you can listen to that shit if you want to!"

His spit landed on my bottom lip.

My knees buckled, and I gripped the side of the stove. He had me—I knew that I wouldn't throw the hot rice. I tried to fight back the tears, but they squeezed out of my eyes anyway. The fear was real. I hated him and I hated myself for being scared of him.

"You need to be your own damn woman!" he screamed, his veins popping out on both sides of his neck. I don't know why you crying, ain't nobody gonna hit your fuckin' ass!"

"Russell, you didn't have to call me a bitch," I whined.

"Fuck you Brenda," he said before backing away from me and leaving the house.

I stood there in shock. I couldn't believe we were back at this point again, that even without getting high his abusive behavior was still present. But mostly I was disappointed that I was still playing his victim. This had to end.

Before I could get caught up in self-pity I remembered Rusty. I ran into the living room to find my son on his knees, his head buried inside his school bag. My God, what must he have been thinking?

Memories of all the shit we'd put Kelisha through made the pain of a frightened Rusty even worse. He wasn't crying, but I could see the fear and confusion in his little face. I picked him up and told him I was sorry and that it would be okay, only to remember I'd said the same thing to Kelisha all of her life and things still weren't okay.

I prayed that when Russell returned that night things would be better. His pattern in the past had been to return, act like nothing happened, have sex with me and fall off to sleep. I was wrong.

"I wasn't gonna hit you tonight. You need to stop acting like you're scared of me," he said as he undressed. He offered no apology for his behavior.

"You wanted to," I said, my back to him.

"That's bullshit."

"Russell, what do you expect me to think?"

"Well shit, you can't be talkin' to me anyway you wanna," he answered.

"And you can call me a bitch?" I asked.

"Forget it."

But I couldn't, even after we had sex.

The next morning on my way to work I made my decision. I was leaving him. I arrived at work and called him.

"I don't know what's happening between us, but I'm going to my mother's.

"I understand."

"I'm gonna take off work tomorrow and come get the car so I can get some of my clothes."

"Alright."

For the first time Russell didn't try to stop me from leaving him, and that in itself was progress. I'm sure he, too, knew this marriage had exhausted itself.

I made arrangements with Eve to pick up Rusty after school while I was gone. I then called my mother and told her I was coming up and didn't know how long I'd be there. All she wanted to know was if Russell had hit me.

The next day I went to Rusty's school, where I sat crying in the auditorium as I watched his special assembly program. Afterwards I went to his first grade class and the teacher let him come into the hallway.

"Hi Mom!" my son exclaimed, excited to see me outside his classroom.

I bent down on my knees so I could be at eye level with him.

"Mommy needs to talk to you," I said, brushing back his curly hair.

He nodded.

"I'm going to stay with La-La and Pop-Pop since Daddy and I are having some problems."

"When you coming home?"

"I don't know yet, maybe on the weekends but definitely when school gets out for the summer," I said, not sure if that were true.

He was smiling like he understood, like I was just going away for another visit with his sister.

I attempted to swallow the lump in my throat before I continued.

"Rusty, Mommy loves you."

His face brightened with a smile. "I know Mom, I love you too," he said, then reached out and gave me a hug.

My heart broke into pieces.

chapter seventeen

Tastes Like Candy
Summer, 1989

Being separated from Russell was like a roller coaster ride for me. As much as I enjoyed it, I missed our being together as a family. Hell, I even missed Bear. There was a lot of back-and-forth on the weekends with the car, the children and with each other.

When I started going to meetings and becoming a part of the social life of NA, I began to hear rumors that there was another woman in Russell's life, so I began to date other men. I'd never go anyplace where I might be seen, but I was out enough to receive the attention I enjoyed from other men, most of whom weren't in the fellowship. But regardless of who I dated, I only had sex with my husband because neither of us were ready to admit that our marriage was over. The other freedom I enjoyed was being able to spend my money the way I wanted to especially since I didn't have to share the expense of the house with him. It was rather selfish because had I been the one left with the house, I would've still expected him to share in the expenses. But I reasoned that he was a man and it was his job to be responsible.

Loving the taste of freedom, I took it a step further. Without Russell's knowledge, and making the children promise to keep it a secret, I got my own apartment. Once again this was a bad decision because what came along with the three bedrooms on Battersby Street were roaches. Had I had taken my parents advice and stayed with them, I would've been okay. But living on top of a pizza shop I should've expected nothing better.

It wasn't hard to keep this from Russell, because he too was enjoying his own freedom. But my secret didn't last long, because when my frivolous spending caused me to be unable to meet the financial demands of having my own place, it was Russell I called on to supplement my paycheck.

Then I finally met someone in whom I took a real interest. I'd noticed the 6'-tall, dark, and sturdily built Gerald around the meetings, and he always had an aura of mystery about him. This night I was at a house party, and Russell had just left, so for most of the night we inconspicuously watched each other. Later, when I went into the basement, I found Gerald standing against the wall, talking to the DJ. I took a seat after dancing; when Gerald came and sat next to me, he was close enough for me to damn near taste his Obsession cologne.

"So, what's up with you?" he asked.

"Nothing," I answered trying to control my interest.

He didn't try to hide the fact that he was checking me out.

"Where did your brother go?"

"What brother?" I asked, puzzled as to who he was referring to.

"You know, Russell."

I laughed—it wasn't the first time we'd been mistaken for siblings.

"That's not my brother, he's my husband."

"Get the fuck outta here! I always thought he was married to that tall skinny yella girl and you were his sister."

I laughed again.

"No, the yella girl is his sister, Jena."

"So how come you two aren't together?"

"You noticed that?"

"That's my job."

"What?"

"I'm a behavior counselor. I notice these things."

"Interesting."

162

"Well we're separated."

"And where are you living?"

Through our conversation we realized that we both lived in the Northeast only one neighborhood apart. By end of the night we exchanged phone numbers with the promise of a date.

Neither the men I dated, nor the possibility of getting to know Gerald helped when I saw my husband with another woman.

It was July 4th, and I was driving down Lancaster Avenue after a barbecue. I drove past 52nd Street and I saw Russell coming out of the house with her. I should've turned around and confronted them both, but I was too stunned to make the u-turn. Instead I decided I'd first find out who she was, and that happened soon.

I'd gone to a meeting that following Sunday in Logan, and the young petite, light- skinned girl wearing a baseball cap was sitting among those in the audience. My idea was to make sure she knew who I was, so I raised my hand to share and spoke about how much I loved my husband and about the toll the separation was taking on me. My tactic worked, because she stood up and walked out. Later, as I was leaving the meeting, she was walking past me. I stopped in front of her, gave her a hug and said, "Hi, my name is Brenda."

She returned the greeting with a nervous hug, never introducing herself—making it obvious that she was the girl with whom my husband was having an affair.

I left that meeting and went to another at Pulaski and Manheim, which had now become my home group. That was where I ran into Gerald. We were standing outside talking when she walked by.

"Who's that girl?" I asked him, pointing to my competition.

"Is that the girl your husband is fucking?" he asked with a smirk.

I nodded my head yes as I looked her over, wondering if it had been her youth that had attracted my husband.

"Her name is Candy. You mean to tell me he's giving you up for her? I don't believe that shit," he answered, squeezing my hand in his.

"What does that mean?"

"I don't know, she's just a regular girl. I think she works at a day care. Not much competition when it comes to your big job at IBM."

I wanted to tell him that was exactly the girl my husband needed, one who would help him stop feeling insecure that I worked in corporate America and he spent his days in a factory.

Not wanting her to catch me staring, I asked him, "Can you walk me around the corner to my car?"

"You know Brenda, you're gonna need to start thinking about yourself and not about what he's doing," he stated.

"I know, but you don't know half the story about my crazy marriage."

"Well, when you get at least one foot out the door, you give me a call and then I'll know you're ready for me."

I drove to Russell's afterwards where I accused him of fucking Candy. He denied it, then he fucked me. Afterwards he was persistent that we get back together until I agreed that was what I too wanted. All I really knew was that I didn't want another woman to have *my* husband.

Russell and I then began spending all our time together, mostly at my apartment. The children loved it, because now we were back to being a family, even if we were slightly dysfunctional. After dinner one night at Blue Point on Harbison Avenue, I decided that we needed to make a statement to those in both of our social circles that we were back together. We agreed to meet that weekend at the Regional NA Convention.

I went down to the center city Holiday Inn that Friday night, to meet Russell but he didn't show that night or the next. He also didn't respond to any of the messages I left on his phone. I was puzzled as to where he was, because I'd actually thought we were serious this time. It didn't go unnoticed to me that Candy wasn't at the convention either.

It wasn't until Sunday afternoon that I finally heard from him.

"What's going on Russell?"

"I'm leaving in the morning to go to Colorado to visit my uncle, and after that I'm going to California to visit Toya and Lena," he stated.

"What? You didn't tell me anything about that! And where the fuck you been all weekend?"

"I been around."

"You're full of it. I mean on Thursday we decide that we're definitely getting back together, we agree to meet at the convention and then you don't show up. So no I'm sorry but you haven't been around."

"I had a lot of thinking to do, so I went to Wildwood with Juan and his girlfriend."

"You did WHAT?"

"Brenda I needed some time by myself."

"Yeah right and who did you take?"

"Nobody. I needed to get away."

"Did Candy get away with you, too?"

"Ain't nothing happening between me and that girl. Look I'll be up there tonight to see y'all."

"Well bring some money because the kids are here and we need some groceries." Late that night he arrived at the apartment while the children were sleeping. We went into the living room to talk.

"Did you bring some money?" I asked.

"Here," he said, handing me two big bags of candy for the kids.

"They can't eat this shit. Russell, what the hell is going on with you?"

"Nothing," he answered very nonchalantly.

"Bullshit! I wanna know where you been all weekend."

"I told you I was with Juan in Wildwood," he answered, slumping down in a chair.

"And you telling me you didn't take anybody?" I asked as I rose from the couch and began pacing the floor.

"Fuck no. The woman whose house we stayed at was trying to get with me but I wasn't fucking her."

I could read that ole lying-ass look in his eyes.

"But what about us and our decision to get back together? I mean, you forgot that we were supposed to meet?"

"Brenda, I had to think things through."

"What else was there to think through? I mean, you could've at least called and told me you weren't going to meet me."

"Listen, all I know is that I'm going to the West Coast and when I come back I want us to get back together."

"Oh, you think it's that simple. I waited for you, the kids waited for you, I called you all weekend with no response, do you know how I felt?"

He paid me no attention as he'd gotten up from his chair and was following me into the kitchen. I knew what was next.

"Com'on why don't you stop all that talking," he said while pressing his body against mine." I'm here now."

"Get the fuck away from me Russell."

The next thing I knew he'd thrown me to the floor and was trying to take what he wanted. There was a part of me that was saying, "What the hell, he was going to get it anyway." But I'd grown, if only a little bit, and this time I fought back, scratching, punching and trying to knee him in his groin until I ripped his herringbone chain from his neck.

Surprised and frustrated he jumped up and said, "You wanna know everything? Well, I'm gonna tell you everything."

I sat up.

"Brenda, there have been a lot of women. I didn't fuck all of them but I been out there."

I was stunned. Here was my husband who'd denied every affair I'd ever accused him of, and now he wanted to tell the truth. I wasn't sure I was ready to hear it all, but it was too late.

"It's been like this. I been spending time with women, but it wasn't just me; it was my friends, too. We'd hang out at the meetings and, you know, we were having fun. That's why I was always coming home late."

"Believe me I felt like shit when I'd come in at two or three in the morning after being with another woman and have to get into bed with you. I knew it wasn't right, but it was like I couldn't help it."

"What about me, Russell? Wasn't I enough?"

"Brenda I love you, you know that, but it was different. They made me feel good, you know? They thought I was something."

"And I didn't?"

"Listen I know I fucked up, but when I get back I swear I still want us to get back together. All I want is my family back."

"So, who did you go to Wildwood with?"

"Just Juan and his girl."

"And what about Candy?"

"Do you really want to know?"

"Yeah."

"I met Candy at our first NA convention. We've been talking for a while and she really is a nice person. I mean, she's been helping me through our separation."

"Was she the one you were coming out of the house with on July 4th?"

"Yeah, but we didn't do anything. I didn't have sex with her until you moved out. Look, she knows I want my family back and I told her it was over."

"And what did she say?"

"She said she understood. I know I hurt you Brenda but—"

"Hurt? I'm fucked up! Why another woman Russell, after we've come so far? Didn't all that shit we went through mean anything?"

"Brenda, once you were gone I realized I didn't even like her as much I thought I did. She was a distraction, someone to talk to."

He continued to talk about his transgressions in between confessing his love to me. His excuse was that at 34 he was getting older, and when these other women began to show interest, it excited him.

I began to cry, and he tried to hold me, but it didn't help. Instead he guided me into the bedroom.

I lay there, stiff, as he passionately tried to make love, whispering in my ear all the things that used to make me forget the other women and the abuse. This time, though, there was one thing missing: I wasn't high.

"Get off me," I finally told him.

"What?"

"GET OFF!"

He rolled over and lay beside me.

"What's wrong?" he asked, lying there holding his now half-hard dick.

I cleared my throat. "Russell, I can't take another woman."

He didn't respond because he knew how many women he'd put me through in the 12 years we'd been together: Lena, Karen, Crystal, Yasmeen, Tia, Jackie, Carla, Pam, Sandy, Angela, and the countless others I couldn't recall or didn't know.

I stared at my handsome husband, the lover of women, and hated him and all of the years I'd wasted. I realized he would never change. Here he was telling me all this shit and now he was leaving for the West Coast. I hated him and I hated recovery. How could a person come this far in their life and still feel so much pain?

"Brenda, what do you mean?"

"I mean, you told me you've been fucking another woman and I'm supposed to go on like nothing happened?"

"Why do you have to say it like that?" he asked, as if there were a better way to put it.

"Say it like what?"

"That I fucked another woman."

"What do you want me to say, that you made love to another woman? Does that make it feel better?"

"All I know, Brenda, is that I love you, and I want my wife and family back. I love you and I need to know if we're gonna get back together when I return."

"Russell, I honestly can't even consider that right now."

The next morning, after dropping the kids off at Rocky Falls Camp, and Russell at Philadelphia International Airport, without planning to I drove to the house on 52nd Street. Climbing the stairs to our bedroom, I knew that as much as I'd hated that house it had become my home. I sat on the bed and looked at the dresser where I knew my perfumes would never again sit. I opened the drawers to see where my clothes used to be folded. That's when a pink envelope with Russell's name written on it caught my eye. There was no doubt it was from a woman.

Rambling through his things, I found more empty envelopes. Then I found a few pages of notes he'd written to himself. Initially I thought I didn't want to read them. Realizing that it was still my house and that another bitch's shit shouldn't be in it, I began to search for the cards that came from those envelopes. I knew where Russell hid things, so I went to the closet that had never had a door and looked inside his suit pockets. There I found the cards. I opened them and read a card whose words were from a woman in love with a man she couldn't have. On the inside she'd written about how hard things were between the two of them, but was shouldn't worry, because they would work themselves out. I saw her name signed at the bottom, "Love, Candy."

Then I decided it was time to read his notes. Hell, he'd read mine enough times. In his journal he revealed how once again his dick had gotten him in trouble. His words spoke about how he knew he was losing me, but he didn't know what to do. I almost felt sorry for him. But then I also read about how much he loved Candy and that it had been love at first sight when he met her.

The ringing phone interrupted me. It was my mother-in-law. I told her what I'd found.

"You only made it worse, Brenda," she said. "Russell loves you and he wants to make things work, 'cause he knows that he fucked up."

"He's hurt me one too many times Eve."

"He wouldn't have told you those things if you hadn't asked," she said, making it was obvious he'd told her about our conversation.

Damn this woman, she'd been in every aspect of our relationship and marriage. When was I gonna learn?

chapter eighteen

Personal Therapy
August, 1989

Gerald, who was now well aware of my deteriorating marriage phoned me one morning at work and invited me to lunch. I was more than eager to go out with him—hewas always able to say the right things. That afternoon we dined at Owens Soul Food Restaurant in the Strawberry Mansion Shopping Center. He was very much the gentleman, opening and closing doors, stepping aside for me to pass, pulling out my chair and allowing me to order first. It was during this lunch that he shared with me about his life. He talked about his childhood, told me that he practiced Islam, confessed that he'd come into recovery via a heroin addiction, and said that he'd also been a pimp. He told me about the women he'd dated in the fellowship and the woman who he was no longer involved with, but who claimed to be carrying his child. None of his lifestyle affected me because I had no interest in being in a relationship with this man. We were just two people having a good time together.

"You know, you should think about coming down to the NA World Convention in Orlando at the end of the month" he said."It'll be a good getaway for you."

"Gerald, I don't have that kind of money right now," I said, having just gotten a promotion and a raise, but also realizing that a vacation with another man was out of the question.

"Listen, if you can get there I'll pay for everything else."

"Are you serious? You don't even know me that well."

"I know enough to see a woman that needs a break from her life."

"I guess you're right about that. Do I have time to think about it?"

"Take all the time you need, I'm waiting on you."

It was nice to know somebody thought I needed a break from the confusion in my life. I doubted, though, that I was bold enough to go that far with Gerald, even if he was footing the bill.

I did agree to meet him at a pool party that weekend at the YMCA on Broad and Master Streets. I'd been there about an hour and was having a pretty good time until I found myself staring at a bikini-clad Candy. She was sitting by the pool with her girlfriends laughing and talking. How dare she be so carefree while I had to carry the burden of knowing how much my husband loved her. Feeling jealous, and knowing that even if I was fool enough to approach her I couldn't take on her entire group, I decided to leave.

I was headed toward the door when I saw Gerald, surrounded by people who seemed to like whatever it was he was saying. Upon noticing me he excused himself and walked over, gripping me in a tight embrace that almost lifted me off my feet.

"Are you alright? Did you see Candy?" he asked.

"Yeah, I'm ok." I lied.

"Look, whenever you're ready I'll give you a ride home."

Comforted by Gerald's presence I decided to hang out for a while. After the party, though, I happened to be standing by the door as Candy walked past. My initial reaction was to slap her, but instead, I was struck with the reality that the tables had turned—this was exactly how my cousin Lena must have felt about me.

I was glad to be seen leaving with Gerald that night, because I wanted Candy to know that two people could play her and Russell's game. Once in the car, Gerald kept his arm around me. For some reason, I felt safe. Being so close, it was hard not to feel sexually attracted to him. I knew he felt the same way, because he kept commenting on my long legs and looking at them like he wanted them wrapped around him

"Look Brenda, everything will be alright, I'm here with you." He reassured me.

"I don't know why I'm so comfortable with you; I don't even know you like that," I told him.

"Hey, it's because that's my purpose in life, to make sure you're okay."

Gerald's words sounded good, but it was way too early to trust this man.

Two weeks later, Russell had gone from Colorado to Los Angeles and we still hadn't spoken except for the message he'd left telling me how much he loved his family.

I'd been assigned to work at a four-day IBM offsite meeting at the Hershey Hotel at Broad and Locust Streets, which helped to keep my mind off that situation. They reserved a room for me and I brought along Rusty and Kelisha.

I'd been at the hotel for two nights when I finally returned a call to Gerald, who'd left a message sounding concerned that he hadn't heard from me. When I spoke to him he'd thought that Russell had come back and that I was running from him. I told him I was okay and that I was staying at the hotel because of my job. It was also during that late night conversation that sex became a topic when he asked me what I liked to have done to me and what I liked to do. I didn't know what to say. I had never been asked that question. I lied and told him that I hadn't been with anyone except my husband for years, so I wouldn't know what I liked. He though, had no problem letting me know how he liked to slowly make love to a woman until he learned her body and what she liked.

That Wednesday night I went to a meeting at 16th and Girard, where outside the meeting Gerald made me the center of his attention, exclaiming to everyone that I was his woman.

"Do you still have your kids at the hotel with you?" he asked.

"Of course," I answered.

"One of these nights you're gonna have to get rid of them."

"Why is that?"

"My guess is a woman like you is going to need someone to hold her tight one of these nights."

Damn, he knew what to say. "Mmmm . . . maybe, I don't know."

The next day I sent the kids to my mother's, because I did need a break. When I checked my messages at home, Russell had called, saying that he was back in Philly. I was tempted to call him, but instead I called Gerald and invited him to the Hershey.

It was a rainy night when Gerald knocked on the door of my hotel room. Peering through the peephole, I didn't expect to see his dark, sexy shoulders. Once he settled on the couch and I sat in the chair facing the television, I ordered some snacks and we watched television and talked; mostly he asked me about my marriage to Russell. He wanted to know about the abuse, and I described some of the beatings Russell had laid on me. Eventually, he said, "I don't want to hear anymore. I mean, what kind of man could beat a woman like that? What is he, a faggot?

"I doubt that," I answered in defense of my husband.

"Why did you stay with him through all of that?"

"Gerald, that's a questioin I just can't answer."

All of the conversation had drained me, so I excused myself to take a shower. While standing under the water I asked myself if I was ready to give myself to this man. Would it mean anything to either of us? Would I regret it afterwards? Wrapping a towel across my breasts and another around my waist, I returned to the sitting area, where Gerald had turned out the lights and tuned the television to a suspense movie. He motioned for me to cuddle under his open arms.

I felt the heat rising between my legs but dared not make the first move. I was practically laying between his legs and couldn't feel his dick, so I figured either I wasn't turning him on, or—even worse—his dick was exceptionally small. He caressed me with one finger, up and down my neck and in my hair, his thick hands, calloused with scars from his heroin addiction, massaged my shoulders.

I wanted him to take me but Gerald was being patient.

Finally I turned and he kissed me until it was one kiss too many. With his strong arms he picked me up and carried me to the bed where I lay watching him undress. His chest was full of curly hair, and when he took off his briefs, his dick sprang out like it was looking for what it was about to enjoy.

As magical as everything was, it didn't lessen the fact that there was a low rumble in my belly; I was afraid that at any moment Russell would come kicking in the door. But feeling so safe with Gerald, I told myself not to worry, that he wouldn't let anything happen to me.

At first I was embarrassed when Gerald completely removed the towels, but my insecurities diminished with the way his eyes feasted upon me. Slowly, with his mouth, he made love to my entire body until I practically began begging him to take me, and he did. For the first time I allowed myself to be enjoyed without having to give anything in return. When our moment was over, his hairy chest lay against me.

"Damn, what have you done to me?" he asked.

"What are you talking about?"

"Shit, no wonder your husband is fucked up."

He walked across the room to his leather pouch, lit a cigarette and sat on the side of the bed puffing on it.

I smiled and didn't say anything. Whether he was lying or not, at the moment I didn't care.

"I know you're gonna do the black widow on me."

"What's that?" I asked, not being sure what he was talking about.

"You know—how the female black widow spider mates with the male and then kills him."

I laughed out loud, but thought to myself that he was far from the man I wanted to kill.

"Gerald, seriously, thanks for giving me what I needed, someone to hold onto."

"Anytime you need me."

The next morning while getting dressed, I made the decision to travel to the convention in Florida.

chapter nineteen

Fair Exchange is no Robbery
1989–1990

A few weeks later, I was stepping off of the plane in Orlando, feeling as though I was leaving all of Philly and the things that were happening there behind me. Gerald had arranged for me to share a room with a sister from the fellowship, so it wouldn't be obvious to everyone that we were together. Once I arrived and unpacked, I took a taxi to meet him at the Sheraton Hotel before I lost my nerve.

I walked through the hotel lobby and out to the pool, where I saw him lounging with a few other people from Philly. He immediately noticed me and walked across the pool area to greet me.

"I'm glad you showed up, I was worried you might not make it," he said. The previous night when he'd phoned, I was unable to talk because Russell had been laying next to me.

Russell, whom I'd argued with, yet given in to because I'd felt guilty for having been with Gerald. I also wasn't so sure that I didn't want to resume our marriage because being with Russell was all I knew. Now we'd moved to a level playing field and this time it was me telling him that I'd make my decision when I returned from Orlando.

Gerald took good care of me over the weekend, and as he'd promised it was all at his expense, which made me even more attracted to him. I met his friends and his sponsor and we celebrated his birthday. But no matter what he revealed about himself, there was still a mysterious side to him that I knew he'd never reveal. Gerald's biggest attribute was how he understood my situation, often analyzing and giving me his professional opinion. Some of it I understood, and some words he had to explain. I'm sure it came from his job as a behavior counselor, but he continually questioned the choices I made. Sometimes it made me wonder if I was more of a patient then a potential girlfriend. Even still, he was able to deal with my fragile emotions at the time, knowing when my mind would drift to my other life, and he'd be right there holding me and consoling me or just making me laugh.

The one vice he had that I didn't like was that he smoked cigarettes; however, my promise to him was that until he stopped I wouldn't perform fellatio. He stopped smoking.

About a week after my return from Florida, Russell came by the apartment. I could tell by his expression when I answered the door that something was wrong. My guess was that he'd heard about my rendezvous with Gerald.

"Brenda, I wanna talk to you," he said, slamming the door behind him.

I led him into the bedroom, because the children were looking at us. I'm sure they were wondering if we were going to start fighting.

"Why, what's up?"

"Who were you fucking in Florida?"

"What are you talking about?" I asked, propping myself against the dresser.

"I heard you were with Gerald down at the convention."

"Bullshit, who told you that? I was hanging out with everybody from Philly."

Russell paced the floor unsure how to control his violent temper.

"Brenda, you know I don't believe that shit. You need to be woman enough to tell me the truth."

"I am telling you the truth."

"You lying! Everybody saw you."

"What was I supposed to do, go down there and hang out by myself?"

"I know you fucked that nigga, didn't you."

"Are you crazy? Get the hell outta here," I said, turning my back to him but continuing to keep my eye on him from the mirror.

That quickly, Russell spun me around, his hands squeezing my shoulders, pushing me around the room.

"Tell me something Brenda, did he fuck you better than I do?"

"Stop it Russell! Don't ask me that. How would I know?" I said, trying to make sure I didn't show fear.

"Don't fuck with me Brenda, you're not gonna embarrass me. I don't want nobody telling me who my wife is fucking."

I only knew one way to tone down Russell's aggressiveness. I lovingly placed my hand on his chest and lowered my voice.

"Com'on why don't you stop talking like that? You know I'd never sleep with another man."

"Yeah right."

I pulled down his zipper. "Russell?"

That was all it took to momentarily take his mind off Gerald, with the exception of his questions during the course of our having sex when he asked who was the better lover, him or Gerald.

When we were finished he picked his pants up off the floor and said, "I hope you don't think that changed anything."

"What do you mean?" I asked, surprised that his anger had returned.

"Fuck you Brenda! I know you fucked that big-head greasy nigga and you gonna pay for it."

"Oh yeah, how's that? What you gonna do Russell, kick my ass?" I asked, now closer to his face than I should've been.

"I'm taking Rusty."

That knocked the breath out of me, he had to be bluffing. He couldn't do that. Rusty was my son.

"What do you mean?"

"You know what I mean, I'm taking *my* son. You ain't gonna be raising him while you fucking another nigga."

He walked out of the bedroom and into the living room where the kids were watching TV.

"Rusty, let's go."

"Where we going Dad?" he asked, still sitting in front of the television with his sister.

"HOME! GET YOUR STUFF!"

Rusty stood up, his eyes on me for clarification.

Realizing he was serious about taking my little boy, I started pleading with him.

"Russell what are you doing? I told you I wasn't fucking Gerald," I cried, grabbing onto his arm with one hand and Rusty with the other, whom he was trying to drag out the door.

He turned with venom in his eyes. "Brenda, you better get the fuck away from me!"

"Russell, don't take my son, *please*. I wouldn't do that to you with Kelisha."

"Did you forget? He ain't your son."

His words stung, because I more than anyone else was aware that Rusty hadn't passed through my womb, but I'd been his mother for the past six years, so how dare he tell me he wasn't mine. I was standing in his face and didn't care if he hit me because I was willing to fight.

"You bastard, how could you say something like that? You're the one who doesn't deserve him. I loved him and cared for him more than his own mother. Hell, probably more than *you*, and you tell me he's not mine? Well fuck you!"

"Brenda, you better get the fuck outta my face."

"Fuck you, you're gonna pay for this you piece of shit."

Not caring that the children were standing on either side of us, he grabbed my face and squeezed until my cheeks felt as if they'd burst.

"If you don't wanna get fucked up Brenda, you better get out of my way," he said between clenched teeth,. He snatched Rusty away from me and they disappeared out the door.

I called out from work the next day, went to Police Headquarters at 8th and Race and filed a Protection From Abuse Order. My next stop was Family Court at 1801 Vine

Street, where I made every attempt and plea to file for visitation and partial custody of Rusty. Their answer was that I had no legal rights to little Rusty Douglass, because I'd never legally adopted him.

Feeling defeated, I pressed on with my relationship with Gerald. In an unrelated step, though, the roach infestation forced me to move out of my apartment. My parents didn't have a problem with Kelisha and me returning to their home on Mill Street, but La-La refused to let me bring any of my roach-infested furniture or bags of clothes. Everything had to be sent to storage.

Up until now I had tried to be careful about exposing Kelisha to my relationship with Gerald, even though she would've clearly understood her mother having a boyfriend. Instead I chose to hide him and would leave the house late at night telling her we were going to dinner. My daughter caught on quickly, because she'd always ask me to bring her a milkshake. So no matter what time I came home I'd have to stop at The Dining Car and pick her up a milkshake; I couldn't bear to break a promise to her.

It was my parents who were the most skeptical of Gerald, especially after the birth of his son, which he admitted was his. La-La kept telling me that Gerald was trying to use me, but I couldn't see it. She'd nicknamed him "greasy," because Gerald kept his hair cut short, almost bald around the sides and back, with a little curly shit on top. The curls, though, were always greasy and so was his face. My Uncle Richard, who lived next door, wanted to know why Gerald only came to pick me up at night. "Nigga must have something to hide."

I ignored all of these signs even as he began to disappoint me. When we would make plans, he'd renege at the last minute, often leaving me and Kelisha disappointed. I even ignored it when I allowed him to use my credit card so he could purchase his son a crib. I'd like to believe that rather than being naïve I just wasn't focused, but how could I be when Russell was putting stipulations on my visits with Rusty.

Since Russell and I weren't having sex, it was rare that I saw Rusty. One evening when Eve came by to bring Kelisha money from Russell, and even though Rusty cried, they wouldn't let him out of the car. I had often thought of calling Gloria to see Rusty, but they'd also turned their backs on me, as had other friends. It was as if everyone had to choose a side and they chose Russell's. Once again I was the "bad girl" for having left my husband.

Russell, though, devised his own scheme for allowing me access to my son—sex for visitation. I often obliged by convincing myself that sex didn't mean anything so long as I saw my son. But it did, and I was just burying my feelings, so I made my last exchange after the holidays.

One afternoon I took a chance and thought if I caught Russell off guard, that he might concede in letting me see Rusty. He agreed. I went to the house and Rusty came to the door, ecstatic to see me. I had to strain to keep from crying. I asked Russell if I could take him to the playground. He agreed as long as we walked. Rusty held my hand and we crossed 52nd Street to the playground. I watched him slide and swing for a while as I searched for the words to say to him. I missed him so much. When I turned and saw Russell watching us from the doorway, I felt like a divorced parent who had to have supervised visits. Did he actually think I would kidnap him?

When I found the words I called Rusty to me and, as he jumped in my arms, the words got trapped in my throat and it was him who said, "Mom, everything is gonna be okay."

chapter twenty

Regeneration
1990

In early Spring rumors started circulating around the office that IBM Philadelphia would be reorganizing. Usually the rumor mill was correct, even if it didn't happen right away. It had already happened in Detroit, however, and it appeared that Philly would be next.

I had no complaints about IBM; they had always been good to me. I made good money, received plenty of overtime and timely raises. God knows I could never thank them enough for putting me and my husband through rehab. Hell, the kids even loved my working at IBM. Every summer there were family outings and every Christmas a holiday party where they were treated to expensive gifts. Who'd want to give all that up?

One Friday afternoon all employees were told to report to a meeting at the Franklin Plaza Hotel where they announced that Area 7 (Philadelphia) would be reorganizing, resulting in a major downsizing of personnel. Here we had people who'd been with IBM over 30 years and now they were facing un-employment from a company that had never laid an employee off and rarely fired one.

There were choices that included relocating to another city, taking a buyout, or bridge to retirement for those who were eligible. We also had the option of remaining in Philadelphia to see where the chips fell. It was Laney who suggested that I consider relocating to Washington, D.C., where there were numerous secretarial openings. The reality was that if I were going to obtain the elite secretarial status at IBM as a Senior Executive Secretary, then a move would have to take place.

Next, I talked to my parents. Surprisingly, they thought a move might be what I needed. I'm sure they were hoping that it would finally free me from Russell.

Kelisha, on the other hand, was totally against it. It wasn't hard to understand why. In her 12 years she'd been uprooted more than the average gypsy, and now here I was about to move her out of the state, again.

Before I could make a decision about relocating, other things happened. La-La called me at work one day to tell me I'd received some documents from a lawyer's office.

"Open it up," I told her, certain someone was suing me for an unpaid bill.

She began to read, "Russell Douglas vs. Brenda L. Thomas in—"

"Mom, are you telling me he sent me divorce papers?"

"Bones, you're right, that's what it looks like."

I was insulted. How could he do this to me? I was the one who had left; I should have been doing the filing. For as much as I thought I didn't want to be with him, I'd always enjoyed the fact that he wanted me. I often thought his being miserable was my way of finally getting back at him. But now I had to face the fact that maybe Candy meant more to him then he was letting on.

The person I did call was Gerald, who picked me up from work that evening. We went to Dante and Luigi's for dinner in South Philly, where I dismissed some of the shady characters he seemed to know. After ordering and making small talk I told him Russell had filed for divorce.

"So, how are you with all this?" he asked.

"A little numb, I guess. He has a lot of nerve asking me for a divorce. Shit, he was the one caught fucking around," I blurted out.

184

"Are you going to sign the papers?"

"I really don't know yet."

There was part of me that wanted to sign them so I could say to hell with Russell. But I was reluctant because I wasn't sure I wanted to be divorced. Divorce meant that I'd failed, that what everyone had said about us not making it was true, that getting off drugs hadn't been the miracle answer to making our marriage work. To tell the truth, I really didn't know how to live my life without him.

Regardless that Russell was seeking a divorce I did have some concerns about how my move would affect his relationship with Kelisha as well as mine with Rusty. When I spoke to him about the relocation he felt it was the worse thing I could do, separating him from his daughter, but he rarely saw her as it was. But he too had moved on. He and Rusty were living with Eve until they could get settled and I'd heard Candy share at meeting that her and Russell were trying to have a baby. It didn't stop me though from feeling jealous that he was, maybe he really did love this other girl but I told myself that one day I too would find love.

But with all that I was looking forward to what would become an adventure, a new life. It was a place that was all mine, where I could do what I wanted. I could make lemonade with real lemons and write without the fear of being beaten that loomed over me, and if I wanted, I could maybe even write a book. There were truly unlimited possibilities now that I was free from Russell.

The time approached quickly for me to make a decision as to whether I would apply for a job in D.C. or stay put in Philly. I also still had the unsigned divorce papers staring at me every morning and night from atop my parent's dining room table. Everyone had weighed in and was waiting for my decision.

On June 28, 1990 I signed the divorce papers and IBM's relocation request. And the next morning Kelisha and I left for a week's vacation in Miami.

Miami proved to be a relaxing time for me and my daughter. We rode Ocean Drive in our rented red convertible and dined at expensive restaurants around the city, spending most of our days either by the pool or on the beach.

Halfway through our stay, I spoke with our hotels concierge and made reservations for us to drive to Key Islamorada, where we would spend two nights at the Holiday Isle Resort.

During the scenic drive down US Route 1, through the everglades, I never gave a second thought to the fact that I was on my own. Some things you just do. That two hours was a real wind-in-your-hair episode, and the words from Pleasure's song, "Joyous" kept playing in my head: "throw away your troubles and leave your blues behind/free your frustrations and have a jamming good time/and let yourself unwind."

Key Islamorada was beautiful. We ate, lounged on the beach, and bought souvenirs. My daughter and I bonded in a way we never really had, because we'd never had time alone, quality time that wasn't overshadowed by drama in her mother's life. She had my full attention. I remember her running from the beach to the pool, taking pictures in her favorite Black Barney t-shirt while her mother sipped virgin pina colada's poolside.

Upon my return to work, Laney told me that there were two openings in the Washington, D.C. area. One was in downtown D.C., at 18th & K Streets, and the other was in Bethesda, Maryland, both holding the title of senior secretary, which would make me one step away from executive.

I traveled to D.C. by train the following Sunday for my interviews and stayed at the Holiday Inn on Rockville Pike. Early Monday morning I interviewed at our offices on Rockledge Drive. The position was to support five mid-level managers. The responsibilities seemed manageable enough, but the clean and serene suburbs didn't have enough pizzazz for me. What would I do at lunchtime? Where would I shop? How would I get around? I tabled that until after my interview in D.C.

By 11:00 a.m. the taxi had whizzed me through Washington, D.C., which was like being in center city Philadelphia. There were shops, traffic, restaurants, people rushing about and I was able to see myself in the middle of it all. Maybe it wasn't quite as fast as Philly, but a minor slow down was its benefit.

There I interviewed with Colleen, the administrative manager who explained that my responsibilities would be to manage the calendar, travel and meeting arrangements for Regional Manager, Gary Adelstein—all things with which I was familiar.

Two weeks after my interviews Laney told me that I'd been offered both positions. Without hesitation I chose the position in D.C. It was then suggested by Colleen and Laney that I return to D.C. for a week of training prior to my relocation.

The biggest decision in all of this was whether or not to take Kelisha with me. My options were to move down there alone, having Kelisha join me the following September before she entered high school or take her with me when I left in three weeks. I knew it might be easier without her, especially since she didn't want to go, but I was tired of leaving her behind, and I didn't want to be alone. Gerald helped me with that decision. He pointed out that Kelisha had always been in and out of my life, always waiting for me to "get myself together." This time she needed to be part of that process.

On August 1st I left for training. I stayed at the Embassy Suites, where I was able to walk to the offices at 18th and K. During my week of training things came easy, as IBM was a corporation that believed in consistency, making my skills easily transferable. Colleen, knowing that I didn't have any friends or family in the area suggested that I meet Kim Gerald.

I called Kim on the phone and she invited me to meet her in the 4th floor smokers' lounge.

The vending room where the smokers were huddled was filled with the stench from their cigarettes and in the midst of it, puffing on a Newport, was the short and shapely Kim Gerald. She had on a black skirt and white blouse, her head crowned with a tight afro.

I'm sure I must have looked very corporate that day in my blue skirt suit, pumps and dark pantyhose. Mostly, though, I noticed that Kim was staring at how very tall I was.

"Hi Brenda, com'on sit down," she motioned, stubbing out her cigarette.

"Hi Kim, thanks for talking to me."

"Oh girl, I don't mind. Colleen told me you moved down here."

"Well not yet, I'm training this week. How long you been down here from New York."

"Me and my daughter been here about a year."

"You relocated with the job."

"No, I just needed to get away from New York," she said, making me wonder if like me she had some demons to shake.

"So Kim, how do you like it here? It's gotta be so different from New York."

"It is, but it's been a good move for me."

"Where do you live? In Washington?"

"I live in Silver Spring, Maryland. Montgomery County has the best school system. My daughter, Barbara is in high school there."

"I guess I could handle living in the suburbs if I'm working in the city everyday."

"Well here's my phone number. If you need help with anything let me know," she said, writing her home phone number on the back of a matchbook.

The major adjustment for me was I didn't know the culture in Washington, D.C.; to me it was the South, so I wondered how I'd get along with my co-workers. Who would I socialize with? I knew nobody. I was going into a foreign land. What about friends for my daughter, how about schools? Who would assist me with making these decisions? I realized it had never been Russell before, and it wouldn't be him now. Then there was the issue of money. Financially my father had always been my money-in-the-bank when I needed or wanted something, but in D.C., 150 miles and two-and-a-half hours from Philly, I was totally on my own.

During the week a realtor took me to look at several condos, townhouses and apartments for rent. On Thursday I chose a two-bedroom rancher on Terrapin Road surrounded by a quarter acre of land in Wheaton, Maryland. It would be perfect for Kelisha and me.

Gerald did as he promised and showed up at my hotel on

Friday night. I treated him to dinner at Phillips on the waterfront. The next afternoon he had business in D.C. so we went to an NA meeting in Southeast Washington, where he introduced me to several women who promised to look out for me.

I had so much to do before moving. IBM was giving me $10,000 in relocation expenses and would put me up at a hotel until I moved into my house. The only furniture I had was a bed for Kelisha and my bedroom set. I was a bit paranoid, because I didn't think I'd be able to rent an apartment or house because of my recent bankruptcy.

As much as I'd secretly dreamed of what it would be like to not have to live under the pressure of Russell, I wasn't quite sure how to deal with it. But sure or not, I was here and I kept telling myself that God hadn't brought me that far to drop me.

The plan was to stay at the Holiday Inn in downtown Silver Spring for a week. My niece, Erica, came with us, because my parents were coming in a week, along with my Uncle Richard who would follow in the u-haul with the remainder of my things.

On August 17, 1990 we packed up a rental car to start our trip south. Kelisha sat sniffling in backseat, uncertain of her own future, while we said our tearful goodbyes to La-La and Pop-Pop. It had been a long time since she'd been this far away from them. But my parents had faith in my ability to be a parent and I prayed I could do right by them.

Driving up the Princeton Avenue ramp onto I-95, I thought about the many moves I'd made; Baring Street, Lindley Avenue, Bustleton Avenue, Viola Street, Charlotte, NC, Market Street, Erdrick Street, Chester, Lyons Place, The Wanamaker House, 52nd Street and Battersby Street. None of them though compared to this one and I prayed that my life in Maryland would hold a better future than my past in Philadelphia.

epilogue

I would love to say that once I moved to Maryland everything in my life was perfect, but there are many lessons to be learned by a woman who had never been on her own. Some of those lessons I gladly welcomed; others I fought off with ferocity. I learned from all of them.

Kim Gerald and her daughter Barbara built a relationship with me and Kelisha that extended far beyond a friendship. We became family. It was Kim who pushed me to gather up the courage to pick up a pen and write about those things that had misshaped my life. Even though I was so many miles away from my past, I'd brought the fear of Russell's warning with me to Maryland. And many nights when I'd sit at the kitchen table, putting my past on paper, I'd hear his threats reverberating in my head and look for him over my shoulder, but I pressed on anyway.

In February of 1991 I received my final divorce decree, but it would take several years before I completely unraveled myself emotionally from Russell Douglass. Not only had I been hooked on drugs, but I was addicted to Russell and the all-consuming lifestyle we'd lived.

As for men overall, I didn't care if I ever married again. All I wanted was someone to be nice to me, someone I could trust not to hurt me. I no longer wanted to feel like I was in bondage in a relationship—I just wanted some peace. Living on my own gave me that.

I remained in Maryland for three years, working my way up IBM's corporate ladder to becoming a successful, senior executive secretary. The corporate community had long offered me benefits beyond pay and healthcare. It was with support and belief from my manager that I'd been able to find rehab and also establish a professionalism that continues to take me far in my career.

When I returned to Philly in 1993 I felt it was time to branch out from the corporate world. It was my daughter this time who encouraged me to establish, my own administrative support company, Admin Ink. The new venture took me into a different world—that of sports marketing and in 1995 I went to work as personal assistant to an NBA athlete. Working for that individual helped me to develop a knack for supporting clients who were young, rich and living in the fast lane of life. That position also laid the groundwork for my first novel.

Originally parts of my life were chronicled through some of the fictional characters in my books: the boldness of Sasha Borianni in *Threesome* and *Fourplay*; the complexities and denial of Tiffany Johnson in *The Velvet Rope*; the naiveté of Caroline in *Every Woman's Got a Secret*.

While writing fiction is a love of mine that will not subside, I have often felt the need to tell my own story—both for my self-discovery and in hopes that it can inspire awareness in others.

Ensuring that I never had to move again, I purchased my very first home in 1994 and have since remained a resident of Northeast Philadelphia. I enjoy my plants, my kitchen table and being 'Ganny' to three beautiful girls. I have a close connection with both of my children and my daughter is my best friend.

Sadly, my parents have passed on, leaving me and my family with an expanded legacy that I pass on to my children and grandchildren on a daily basis.

Despite my recovery and newfound strength and success, there are still times when I want to slip back into the person I was. I've learned to fight those moments. I believe that it is not one specific event that causes you to change. Change occurs as a result of many tiny moments that pop up and force you to say, "Oh, so *that's* why I'm like that." The most significant lesson I've learned is that "getting it together" ultimately takes a lifetime.

BRENDA L. THOMAS

laying down my burdens
a memoir

October Is National Domestic Violence Awareness Month

If after reading this book you are still unclear about the meaning of Domestic Violence please read the following:

What is Domestic Violence?
Domestic Violence is a pattern of assaultive and coercive behaviors, including physical, sexual, and psychological attacks, as well as economic coercion, that adults or adolescents use against their intimate partners for the purpose of gaining power and control over them.

Are you being abused?
It can be difficult to acknowledge that you, or someone you care about is involved in an abusive relationship. Domestic Violence does not look the same in all relationships; however, there are some warning signs that may indicate you are in an unhealthy relationship. Take a few minutes to answer these questions:

- Does your partner insult you in public or in front of your kids?
- Does your partner treat you like you are stupid or call you names?
- Does your partner try to control what you do?
- Does your partner act really jealous of your friends and family?
- Does your partner blame you for his/her violence?
- Has your partner ever threatened to hurt you or him/herself if the relationship ends?

The National Domestic Violence Organization
800-799-SAFE
800-787-3224 (TTY)
www.ncadv.org

The Pennsylvania Coalition Against Domestic Violence
800-537-2238 (National)
800-932-4632 (PA)
800-553-2508 (TTY)
www.pcadv.org

Women Against Abuse
866-723-3014
www.womenagainstabuse.org

Narcotics Anonymous
www.na.org

Alcoholics Anonymous
www.alcoholics-anonymous.org